ACQUAINTED W

by the same author

I FLY OUT WITH BRIGHT FEATHERS
TAL NIV'S KIBBUTZ
(a book for children)

ACQUAINTED WITH THE NIGHT

A Year on
the Frontiers of Death

ALLEGRA TAYLOR

SAFFRON WALDEN
THE C.W. DANIEL COMPANY LIMITED

First published in 1989 by Fontana Books, London

This edition published in 1995 by
The C.W. Daniel Company Limited
1 Church Path, Saffron Walden, Essex, CB10 1JP, England

ISBN 0 85207 285 6

Production in association with
Book Production Consultants plc, Cambridge
Printed by WSOY, Finland

For Richard

ACKNOWLEDGEMENTS

Many people helped and encouraged me in the writing of this book, cheered me on when I was flagging and held me when I felt sad. My special thanks:

To all those whose words have inspired me; to all the teachers and healers who so skilfully imparted their knowledge and wisdom; to John Shine and Christopher Spence for their vision of London Lighthouse; to Tracy Wyatt who taught me a lot about good nursing; to the staff of the children's ward at the Middlesex Hospital for their exemplary standards of patient care; to Henry Tennant for living so courageously with AIDS; to Dr Simon Mansfield for kindly checking over the section of the manuscript concerned with the medical facts of AIDS; to Carol O'Brien for her faith in the project; to Amanda McCardie for her brilliant editing; and above all to those people whose final days I was privileged to share and whose stories form such a central part of this book.

I stepped out into the night, my night
And the stars were my stars.
And the only sound was the tide coming in, coming in,
                                    coming in . . .
I am the child of the tide.

The last writings of a 75-year-old women

1

> In the last analysis it is our conception of death which decides all our answers to the questions life puts to us.　　　　　　　　　　DAG HAMMARSKJÖLD

This is a book about confronting death – the old grim reaper, the skeleton in the cupboard. Until it crosses our path we rarely give it a thought. It only happens to the other guy and doesn't concern us.

The account of my first direct encounter with death is such a shameful tale of cowardice and ignorance that although it happened some years ago, recalling the story now still fills me with remorse and mortification. All I can say in mitigation is that it taught me an unforgettable lesson and was the first step, for me, in recognizing how neglected a subject death is and how ill-equipped most of us are to deal with it.

In the village where we have always spent our summers we became friendly with an elderly couple who also came there annually. They'd married late and at just about the last possible moment, Ingrid, then aged forty-six, had given birth to a son. When we first met them the boy was thirteen, adored, indulged and over-protected. Very bright and gifted, he was the embodiment of all their hopes and dreams.

A few days before his fifteenth birthday he was knocked off his bicycle by a hit-and-run driver. He never regained consciousness and died three days later. Ingrid wrote a stark letter to tell me and later I received another short note from her letting me know that her marriage had not survived the trauma. Rather than bringing them closer, the bitterness, feelings of guilt and accusations of blame had torn them apart.

Shocked, I answered the letters with useless platitudes, and because they lived quite a long way from us I never expected to see them again. I was a bit taken aback the following summer, therefore, when I saw Franz all alone, a desolate figure, walking on the dunes by the sea in our holiday village. He didn't notice me and I avoided him because I just couldn't handle the situation. The enormity of his grief and suffering was beyond my comprehension. No one close to me had ever died; I'd never even seen a dead body. I didn't know what to say or how to behave, so I did nothing.

During that month he spent most of the time by himself in his cottage. We caught sight of him once or twice in the town but he seemed deliberately to look the other way. I interpreted this reaction with a certain amount of relief and self-justification as evidence that he wanted to be left alone. So we left him alone.

The moment of truth came near the end of the holiday when I mentioned to a neighbour that Franz didn't seem to want to have anything to do with us. He looked at me reproachfully and replied, 'Have you asked him? Actually he is terribly hurt and can hardly believe that you haven't even been to see him, that you haven't even acknowledged his son's death. He thought you were friends and can't understand how you could have turned your back on him at such a time.'

My face burning, I realized how my own fear and inadequacy had compounded Franz's already intolerable isolation. Afraid of saying the wrong thing or having my sympathy rejected, I had hurt him still further. How stupid, how unimaginative to suppose that not talking about his son would somehow help to take his mind off the tragedy. Obviously he was thinking about nothing else.

In November Franz hanged himself. Maybe nothing could have averted such an outcome, but a more informed and sensitive attitude towards death and bereavement on the part of us and others of his so-called friends might have helped him survive the worst of his grief.

* * *

I only fully understood the lesson when my own father died a few years later. I wanted to talk about him all the time. I wanted to relive and share my memories of him, recount the details of his death, until I'd started to come to terms with them. The number of friends who were able to listen and allow me the opportunity to vent my feelings were very few.

Our culture seems particularly inept. We have nothing with which to help ourselves or help others. Death is seen as unnatural, an outrage, an intruder. It is evaded, ignored, denied. It is taboo, bad taste, morbid, embarrassing. We stay away from terminally ill or bereaved people because of our own unresolved fear of loss and our unbearable, unspeakable feelings of helplessness and despair. We are clumsy and awkward, afraid of causing them more pain. If we are forced to be with them we avoid talking about death, try to take their minds off it, change the subject, cheer them up. A friend of mine whose baby died was told by a well-meaning neighbour, 'Come on, give us a smile. You're lucky to have the other two.'

'Everyone seemed too busy to give me the warmth I craved,' she said. 'I felt I had to be the one to make the first move, to make it all right.'

We live in a society where control of the emotions is highly prized, condemning us, men in particular, to suffer in silence. Another friend, Jane, who had just learned that the lump in her breast was a rapidly growing malignant tumour wrote to tell her family in America. When they wrote back they didn't even mention her cancer. It made her feel invisible – already erased, unmentionable, unclean and terribly alone.

Most non-Western cultures are a lot better at this than we are. They have rites of passage to mark the momentous transitions in their lives, and belief systems that make it easier for people to accept and experience death. In fact many of them see death not as a final obliteration but as a transfiguration – a gateway through which the soul must pass in order to undertake the next part of its journey. Death is a reunion, a homecoming. In many cultures it is seen almost as the spice

11

of life. Without death it would be very difficult to give meaning to life or to attribute significance to personal events or achievements. Life has value precisely because it is transient and impermanent.

This is a very different view of life from our own, where growing old, terminal illness and dying are an unwelcome reminder that we are not omnipotent and immortal, as we would like to pretend. In our youth-worshipping, achievement-orientated philosophy of life there is no place for death. The dying person is a failure, a loser, and the mourner an embarrassment.

Death is the most predictable thing that will happen to me and one of the few experiences that I will share with every other human being, yet I've hardly given it a thought. I feel at the mercy of a medical profession which sees me as a collection of spare parts to be serviced and is committed to preserving life but seriously ill-equipped to give counsel or comfort to a dying person. The church, for me, has become a repository of stale platitudes. In spite of the fact that the subject has opened up considerably in the last ten years or so, largely thanks to the work of Elisabeth Kübler-Ross, there is still a conspiracy of silence surrounding death. Most of us behave as if pretending it doesn't exist gives us a measure of control over it.

When my mother was dying I was pretty useless. My pain and her stubbornness made it very difficult to do anything for her or for any real communication to take place. I drove across town every couple of days to visit her, chewed up with ambivalent emotions – resentment, panic, love, despair; wanting her to live for ever; wishing she'd get it over with. I wish I'd known how to help her better, just to be with her and keep her company. But I was afraid of getting sucked into the role of dutiful daughter that I had tried to escape all my life. Afraid of her power. I couldn't just be myself. She wasn't afraid; I was. She was sustained by a passionate certainty that she was already half-way to being with her beloved again. She was impatient for death but I didn't know how to let her go.

12

She finally died in her little kitchen, alone, watering her plants. This note in her wavery handwriting was on the bedside table:

4.45 a.m. ad infinitum

Glow without a flicker clear and beautiful blue light.
Through the night keep watch over our love that never
                                                    dies.
Penetrate through my heart your clear blue light.
Telling me of our eternal flame
Our eternal love
That will never fade
That glows more brightly
More truly
More surely
As the days slip by
And the nights.
Little blue light that shines through the night
Undying as your love for me – stronger and purer
As the days and nights of my life fade slowly away
Bringing me nearer to you with every failing breath
Of mine.
Oh give me that light to lighten my alighting
From this life
To my life again with you
For ever more.

I was glad for her and moved by the unwavering constancy of her conviction, but saddened and enraged by her wilful neglect of her health and her refusal to perceive life as worth living without my father.

I cried for her little body when we'd laid her on the bed – thin, straggly, grey hair with just a memory of the flaming auburn she was so proud of still left at the ends. Those hands that had stroked us, those breasts that had given us life and comfort, that dear face. Oh God! I didn't know what to do!

13

My secular culture left me shipwrecked, with no maps, no charts, no guidelines for dealing with death. In the Jewish tradition which is my heritage but from which I am estranged, every nuance of behaviour for the mourning procedure is carefully laid down and everyone engages in an elaborate ritual tried and trusted from ancient times – a choreography of response and counter-response. The mourner is part of what has gone before and part of what is yet to come, surrounded and cushioned until the calamity of loss has receded into its proper perspective.

Hawaiians call in the friends and relatives and have a wailing procession followed by a huge feast. The Irish keep the body in the front parlour for three days for everyone to see and have a great wake with crying and laughter, music and speech-making, to pay their last respects and give the dead person a terrific send-off.

But I, as an emancipated, free-thinking Westerner, had nothing to help me, no code of behaviour, no knowledge of procedure. A firm of unctuous undertakers who kept referring to 'your dear departed mother', came and took her body away and a rabbi who didn't know her intoned the funeral service. It was all very bleak. Luckily for me I am part of a large demonstrative family, so we were able to show our feelings with each other, but most of my friends were as awkward and clumsy as I had been with Franz. 'Sorry to hear about your mother,' mumbled one or two, looking the other way. Another left a note on my doorstep but wouldn't come in. I wanted them to say, 'I wish I'd known her better – what was she like?' and listen while I told them.

Germaine Greer once wrote about going to Italy after a bereavement and deciding to dress in traditional black mourning. The effect was marvellous. Everyone she met knew exactly what to say and how to provide a healing environment for her grief. For my part, I just had terrible dreams as my unconscious mind tried to make sense of what had happened. Dreams of airliners crashing, of being asked to play games where I didn't know the rules, of being asked illogical questions and having to wear a brown paper bag over my head until I knew the answers. Dreams of being unable to control the events around me.

I found my way through the maze slowly and painfully in the weeks and months that followed. My brother and sister and I spent days in her flat packing the books, sharing the little possessions amongst ourselves and bundling up the clothes to give away. Then one day I went over there alone to sort through the papers in various briefcases and the drawers of my father's old desk. It was a forlorn task for which I'd steeled myself in advance. I was planning to be brisk and efficient. I kept all the letters, photographs and notebooks and threw away the rest. I was all right until I came to a shoe box full of our old letters to Father Christmas, Mother's Day cards and first baby teeth. An old tissue with the dusty, crumbled fragments of a long-dead flower in it, a pair of yellowed, shrunken, hand-knitted baby bootees, drawings in childish crayon with 'I love you Mummy' scrawled on them. I could feel my anguish rising like vomit, that hysterical feeling of loss and grief that you get when you're five years old and you dare to let yourself imagine the possibility of your mother dying.

I found a little plastic farm animal – a sheep, still stuck with sellotape on to the paper garden with flowers I'd made for him. She'd kept it for forty years. And the dam burst. I started to sob and howl in a way I hadn't since I was a tiny child. I was crying because I was an orphan and my mother was dead and my childhood was really over. I remember feeling that if somebody didn't hold me I would disintegrate; I couldn't contain the overwhelming forces in my body. So I wrapped myself in a blanket and rocked back and forth with my eyes closed, sucking my thumb. I cried until I choked and made myself sick. Then, exhausted, I curled up on the floor in front of the fire and slept.

It was as if I'd been rehearsing this feeling all those years ago when I used to make myself cry thinking about her dead.

15

I'd cry myself to sleep in an exquisite excess of misery. Now it was the real thing.

When I woke up it was dark outside. My face in the mirror looked like a boiled cauliflower or a bad case of the mumps, but I felt curiously peaceful and calm. I knew I had instinctively let myself do exactly the right thing – the catharsis had healed the child in me and I was free to move on. I took a last look at all our little baby things in that box – all those memories of sweet-smelling tenderness. 'Forgive me,' I whispered, and I threw them all away and closed the door behind me.

And now enough time has passed, my edges are not so raw, and I can begin to piece together my thoughts *before* I am engulfed by circumstance again. Out of the work on my book about healing* came the understanding that only when you have faced the dark shadows in your own house can you begin to help others to do the same. Also, that healing as a tool and a way of thinking can be useful to the very end of our earthly existence. I think we need to heal our attitude to death.

Stephen Levine writes in his revolutionary book *Who Dies?*: 'Whatever prepares you for death enhances life. It means being open and ready for whatever happens excluding nothing . . . if you're here now you'll be there then.' Death can be transformed, he believes, from a frightening enemy, a defeat, an unfortunate error of the universe, into 'an adventure to surpass all adventures, an incredible moment of growth, a graduation'.

One of the greatest obstacles to coping with the needs of the dying and the bereaved, it seems to me, is our failure to examine our reactions, fears and fantasies concerning our own mortality. So at the beginning of this year I found myself asking some fundamental questions: How could I learn to

* *I Fly Out With Bright feathers: The Quest of a Novice Healer*, C.W. Daniel.

cope with the unalterable fact of death? With the impermanence of life? Without dwelling on it unduly or living in a
constant state of anxiety, how could I come to grips with the
heart-stopping realization that there was no guarantee that I
would see anyone I loved ever again? The only thing I could
be sure of was that one day, any day, they or I might die.
Youth, goodness, health or fame would not save us, and yet
I'd never talked about the implications of this with anybody.
How could I learn to be more skilful, more useful to a dying
person or a grieving friend? I had no idea even what I thought
about the subject of life after death. Wasn't it time I found
out?

By a fortuitous coincidence, a list of seminars and workshops
from one of the growth and human potential organizations
whose mailing lists I am on came through the post soon
afterwards. Leaping out at me from among the usual classes
on art therapy, creative visualization and so forth was 'Care
of the Dying and their Relatives', a weekend course at RIGPA,
the Buddhist centre in London. I signed up.

Christie Longaker, a serene, softly spoken young American
woman, was the course leader. She had become involved as a
direct result of her own harrowing experience – she had lived
with and cared for a husband with leukaemia, and survived
the devastation and desolation of her grief when he died eight
years ago.

All their worst difficulties, she said, came out of not
knowing. Not knowing what their rights were, not knowing
the likely progression of the disease, not knowing how to speak
with consultants. All the experts took it for granted that she
and her husband would aquiesce to the helpless-victim syndrome. ('Look, it's not your job to worry about what's going
on. Leave that to us. Your job is to be the patient,' a friend of
mine was told by her doctor when she attempted to question
him about her treatment.) But Christie challenged that

17

assumption, determined to become as well informed as possible. What choices did they have? What support could she draw on? What practical skills could she learn? Rather than be drowned by catastrophe, could they not use the time creatively – viewing death as a gift that had brought a new perspective and strength into their lives? Was it possible to learn how to live with an awareness of your own death, how to use life to prepare for death?

In the years since his death, Christie has dedicated herself to disseminating the wisdom they acquired. She joined the growing hospice movement – at that time there were only three hospices in the USA; now there are between three and four hundred – to learn from patients and eventually to teach volunteer courses, suggesting to people a different way to view death.

In the Middle Ages, she points out, death was seen very much as a companion on life's journey. Paintings of the time show people dancing with skeletons, partners in the dance of life. In our time death is portrayed as the enemy, a hooded ghoul with a scythe. But doctors will protect us, won't they? we say, anxiously looking over our shoulders. But they can't protect us from our fear of death, so we have developed the ultimate denial of death, the macabre technology of cryonics, which enables you to have your body deep frozen in perpetuity until science comes up with a remedy for whatever medical oversight it was that caused your death. Trying to freeze the moment for ever is the ultimate manifestation of our inability to let go and move on.

Since death is seen as unnatural and certainly not a part of everyday experience, it is hard for us to treat it with dignity. We've thrown out the concept of what happens after death or of whether consciousness survives death. The idea of the soul's journey tends to be treated as rather pathetic wishful thinking, not compatible with sophisticated scientific observation. But Western science may have been a little premature in its condescending dismissal of ancient systems of thought. Christie has culled many useful insights from the Buddhist tradition

18

in particular, and now incorporates them into her teaching. I found the ideas very exciting and liberating. Maybe our biggest mistake is always trying to make the scale of things too small. By our craze for pigeonholing we constantly diminish the grandeur.

The Buddhists say that the great illusion of life is its seeming permanence. Like a river it is always moving and changing. The origin of fear is the refusal to accept the reality of impermanence. A Buddhist master once said, 'We spend this life preparing, preparing, preparing to live and then we die and meet the next life unprepared. Pigeon spends the whole night making bed and when the dawn comes he has no time to sleep.' In the Buddhist tradition death is very useful and not to be despised. It is the measure of all things. The awareness of death creates Mindfulness – a very desirable state. When you accept that you're going to die you kid yourself a little less. Priorities change; you look at life differently. When you begin to reflect on death you begin to live. It is part of the process of growing up. Sometimes, during those flashes of enlightenment that we occasionally experience, there is a feeling of oneness and timelessness, a sense of a hall of mirrors stretching in all directions to infinity. If we trust this sense of belonging to the eternal river of life, why should we fear death? Our suffering is caused by holding on to how things might have been, should have been, could have been.

Life is a constant succession of changes, small deaths one after the other. Our choice is either to mature with the understanding of that or to try to freeze time and hold loss at bay. Stephen Levine talks about letting go of the protective straitjacket we lock ourselves into: 'To die into the present moment, to live fully with what is given allows you to meet each moment with acceptance and compassion instead of fright.'

Your way of life will influence your view of death, and your view of death will influence the way you die, says Christie, and although of course you can't tell when your death will be, whether or not you keep your integrity then will depend on the life you lead now. If your life has been a succession of blighted hopes, death will be seen as the final disillusionment – 'There, what did I tell you? Just my luck! Everything bad happens to me.' Our distress when facing death grows out of the way we cope with life. All of a sudden the usual mechanisms don't work; denying the unpleasant, blaming others, complex power plays, artificial fronts are no longer effective strategies, and a wave of panic or fear may result. Or there will be great bitterness and resentment at the injustice of an untimely death – our own or that of someone we love – which has robbed us of our plans.

Christie got us to attempt an impromptu drama in which we took it in turns to play the different characters in a death-bed scene: the distraught relative; the voluntary worker; the withdrawn child; the dying person.

As I lay there, my eyes closed, trying to visualize everything I loved receding from me, I knew without a shadow of a doubt that what I most wanted was to be treated as a living person right to the end. To be treated as I always had been, as me. I felt a need to finish relationships and say my goodbyes calmly. I saw myself as weak and frail but with a last great longing to pass on something of value. I wanted someone to put a baby in my arms for me to hold. A last connection with life – a symbol of love and renewal.

From my family I wanted only closeness, an easy honesty and assurances that they would be all right. From visitors I wanted to know that they would provide a support network for the family after my death. I did not want anyone to take heroic measures to resuscitate me or to save my soul. Anyone who spoke to me of spiritual things needed to be supportive of my own beliefs and not a representative of alien ones.

I did rather feel that it was my show, and that the most loving last thing people could do for me would be to set aside their own needs and help me have the kind of death I wanted.

I remembered that when I had done a course with the healer Jack Schwartz in America the year before one of the most interesting ideas he put forward was that 'Meditation is time out for dying' – a rehearsal for leaving the prison of our separateness. In that altered state of consciousness the limitations of being an earthbound creature begin to disintegrate and we experience intimations of our oneness with all existence. We are afraid of the void without recognizing that the void is our true nature.

I have since tried several deep meditations on being the dying person, just allowing myself to dissolve and surrender, to trust the intuitions that come up – to see myself 'through God's eyes', as Levine says; to 'rest in the nature of mind', as Buddhist teaching puts it.

These reflections, flirtations if you like, have brought with them an exhilarating sense of freedom. Even if I never get to play my final scene as an old lady surrounded by my loved ones and get run over by a bus tomorrow instead, I have an ideal – a template which will influence how I behave towards a dying person and how I feel about leaving this world myself.

The more I read the more I keep coming across affirmations from the great spiritual traditions:

> The great truth that we are here to learn is that the Life Eternal is not a state we go to after death but is an inner condition of consciousness to be attained now.
>
> SIR GEORGE TRADESMAN

> The oldest wisdom in the world tells us that we can consciously unite with the Divine while in this body.
>
> RADAKRISHNAN

At the moment of death we face ourselves. My intuition is that it is not God (whatever that means) who judges me; 'God' stands for love, the all-compassionate. The real judge is myself, and the judgement, the coming to terms, the forgiveness will have to come from me. Peace will come with the acceptance of myself and the acceptance of death.

'Death is unpredictable, therefore one is never ready *enough*,' says Sogyal Rinpoche, a Tibetan teacher. 'Make time for

21

yourself because that is all you've got. Not material possessions, not other people. At the end the sum total of your life is the truth of yourself. When you look into death you face the most important things in your life.'

I also feel that a mature contemplation of death will illuminate old age, so that the destination and the getting there are fully integrated. The great Roman philosopher Seneca wrote:

> Rehearse death. To say this is to tell a person to rehearse freedom. A person who has learned to die has unlearned how to be a slave. He is above and beyond the reach of political power. What are prisons or bars or wardens to him? He has an open door. There is but one chain binding us in fetters and that is our love of life. There is no need to cast out this love entirely but it does need to be lessened somewhat so that in the event of circumstances ever demanding this nothing may stand in the way of our being prepared to do at once what we must do some time.

Appreciation of finiteness enriches self-knowledge and propels us toward creativity and achievement.

I am aware that my gradually awakening interest in questions of mortality has a lot to do with growing older. Most of my terror of dying used to be bound up with fears not for myself but for the little orphans I would leave behind. I could take my chances with the great unknown, perhaps, but they still needed a mother. Even with my increasing equanimity, the world without me is difficult to conceive. I remember hearing a television newsreader saying, 'The bodies of two more women were recovered in the Townsend-Thoresen ferry disaster.' 'How anonymous! How undignified! How insulting!' exclaimed my friend Nella. 'Is that it? Two more bodies? What a horrible way to describe them. Imagine if that was us, Allegra and Nella. Just a couple of statistics and then a commercial for lager.'

But life will go on without me, largely unchanged apart

from some sadness on the part of a dozen people at the most. 'How could I not be among you?' wrote a young man dying of cancer. There is no answer to that painful question because clinging on makes the suffering worse. There is only the thought that if we can treat everything that comes to us as a gift, a kind of grace, then we can let it go lightly back into the flow. Since we cannot keep things anyway and nothing stays the same, we can experience it all and give it all away.

I met a young mother at Christie's workshop whose little girl had died of cancer. 'I used to sit in my rocking chair and just rock and cry, rock and cry. My healing came in learning to rejoice in the beauty of the time we'd shared,' she said. 'Her cup was full before mine. Now the rest of us never put off anything we can do together; we may not have another chance.'

Another mother, talking about her son who died of bone cancer said, 'After all the agony we have come to understand that the only way you can really find love is to give it away. Like a smile it returns. He knew that, and we believe that in a way he continues to live on if his best qualities are kept alive by the people who loved him.'

Christie spoke a lot about bereavement. To be bereft is to be robbed, and the act of mourning is the way we process our loss. Few people, until it happens to them, realize how long this can take and how intense the accompanying physical feelings are: shock, numbness, palpitations, depression, confusion, heartache, loss of appetite, sleeplessness. 'Give yourself permission to heal slowly,' she said. 'The deep feelings of loss are cyclical. Don't expect the intensity of them to diminish for a long time.'

I've heard it said that love is the closest emotion to grief, although it might not seem immediately to be so. One is creating the bonds that intertwine you with another human being; the other is dissolving those bonds. It's not unusual for the grieving process to take two years, and it is important for friends and family members to understand that a person may need support quite a long time later.

23

Apart from our tradition of sending letters of condolence, we have alas largely lost the well-defined conventions of mourning which offered a blueprint for acceptable behaviour in grief and also suggested the sort of time scale after which it would be possible to pick up the threads of normal life again. On the other hand, people's need to invent new ways to help each other has given rise to some inspirational examples of courage, love and resilience.

Christie's course helped me begin to understand some of the processes a person may be experiencing in the face of death and some of the ways to help someone through the time of bereavement. In developing tools and skills to use for healing, I had already discovered how effective visualization and meditation could be for getting in touch with what you already know at a deeper level. 'Insight' means exactly what it says – seeing within. It seems that truth doesn't require learning so much as uncovering.

The demand of our science-worshipping civilization that we should be logical and reasonable at all times gradually erodes and eliminates the spontaneous and instinctive ways of knowing we are born with. They are dismissed as a kind of untrustworthy craziness. I am sure that once we lose our precious capacity to be crazy and to experience the spaciousness of our unexplainable feelings, we lose touch with a major part of our inner wisdom.

I felt augmented by what I had learned – much more receptive. I was also perfectly aware that all the theory in the world is a poor substitute for practical experience, so I wrote to Dame Cicely Saunders to ask if I could come and work as a volunteer at St Christopher's Hospice in South London.

The hospice movement has grown rapidly since Cicely Saunders transformed her dream into reality twenty years ago with the opening of St Christopher's, the first teaching and research hospice. Its aim has always been to provide first-class medical treatment and care to all patients for whom cure is no longer a realistic objective and to provide a warm and friendly environment in which a person can live as fully as

24

possible for whatever time is left. Members of the family are welcomed and encouraged and their usefulness is stressed.

As most people fear the pain of terminal illness much more than they fear death itself, the most important challenge to a hospice is to reassure patients and their relatives that pain and other distressing symptoms can be brought under control. Cancer is particularly dreaded because of its widespread association with unbearable pain, which many hospital doctors and general practitioners seem unable effectively to relieve. In a hospice the concept of care shifts from quantity to quality of life so the need to avoid long-term addiction to strong narcotic drugs such as morphine is no longer a top priority.

St Christopher's has led the way in this field and made a lot of pioneering studies into the complex factors that may be involved in a patient's suffering. For example, the fear of agony can in itself cause such anxiety and tension that the pain becomes worse. Psychological distress, anger, isolation, loneliness and family problems may all be contributory factors as well.

Constant pain calls for constant control, the hospice movement believes. It should never be allowed to get out of hand. A large proportion of patients admitted to a hospice are suffering from serious pain on arrival. This can nearly always be eliminated, and it is at this point that the hospice team can begin to unravel some of the factors which may have contributed to it in the first place. There is often a lot of 'unfinished business', to use Elisabeth Kübler-Ross's phrase, to be worked through at this time. People need sensitive help and encouragement to face some of the emotional, spiritual and social aspects of their distress rather than pretend they don't exist.

Unfortunately it's not uncommon for a patient in an ordinary hospital to be told, 'I'm sorry, there's nothing more we can do for you.' At St Christopher's the same patient would be told, 'Everything possible is being done.'

'It is surprising how much can be achieved and how quickly. People in crisis often show an astonishing ability to resolve long-standing problems and even handle new ones,' says Dame Cicely, 'though for some it is a struggle deeply painful to watch.'

Hospices are committed to a policy of honesty without necessarily bludgeoning a person with the stark truth. I have watched this principle in action before, when I spent many days and nights staying in the children's ward of the Middlesex Hospital with my littlest daughter, who was going through the trauma of major surgery. Nothing was ever done to a child until it had first been gently and carefully explained. If something was going to be unpleasant they were warned and told what to expect. They were allowed to make choices wherever possible, ('What time would you like to have your chemotherapy?') and to fill in their own temperature charts. If a nurse said an injection or a blood test was only going to hurt a little bit, they knew they could trust her. If a child was going to have to face the possibility of dying, the opportunity for talking about it was there.

It would be a wonderful thing if this respect for patients were more widespread. Everyone I know has a horror story to tell of being treated like a leg of mutton by a consultant who sweeps in surrounded by his entourage, doesn't bother to introduce himself, talks over your head in jargon you can't understand and proceeds on his way. My cousin, admitted to hospital for a biopsy to determine whether or not a lump in her breast was malignant and awaiting the results, was sitting up in bed feeling apprehensive and miserable when the ward-round posse arrived. The great man picked up her notes, peered at her over his half-glasses, prodded her right breast, turned and announced to his colleagues, 'This is the one that's got to come off.' She told him what she thought of him in colourful English, got dressed and went home. His high-handedness and insensitivity so enraged her that a new determination to cure herself without recourse to mutilation entered her life and propelled her into relinquishing the victim role and becoming much more assertive. This was six years ago: the cancer seems to have disappeared.

The question of honesty and how much to tell is obviously a tricky one. To tell someone more than they can bear is cruel. Not to tell them what they want to know is equally cruel. Avoiding the issue is dishonest and fobbing them off is cowardly. I believe that most people, at some level within themselves, know the truth and will seek confirmation only of what they feel they can cope with. If a person has not been able to look life in the face he may not be able to look death in the face either. He will quite probably leave his life as reluctantly as he has lived it. If the worst comes to the worst, denial, as we all know, is a great anaesthetic against the pain of reality. Ultimately the degree of understanding has to be each individual's choice. If he doesn't want to know, he has a right not to know, and the person with the information has the sacred responsibility to tell as much as he asks for, as much as he wants to know, skilfully and carefully and always with the assurance that he will never be abandoned or left unaided to cope with some physical crisis.

Courage and common sense are the characteristics repeatedly observed and admired by Dame Cicely in her hospice patients. 'When medical staff are honest,' she says, 'patients are more likely to accept reassurances that pain will not be allowed to get out of control and that death itself will be peaceful.'

She had kindly invited me to come and visit her and made a space in her busy schedule for us to talk. She was helpful and encouraging, a lovely woman who seems to have realized her own equanimity through her quiet faith and capacity for unconditional love. In fact, she said, St Christopher's already had a full complement of volunteers, but she suggested another hospice nearer home for me to try.

As with most things in life there was rather a gap between the idealized fantasy and the day-to-day reality. The building was peaceful and the gardens were lovely, but my introduction was not as I'd pictured it. I was interviewed on my first morning by the volunteer co-ordinator, a stick-like woman of desiccated aspect – the archetypal Miss Prim, a perfectly

27

preserved Edwardian fossil. She referred to the volunteers as her 'gels', mentioned that trousers were not considered suitable wear and stressed that although contact and conversation with patients were probably inevitable, any meaningful dialogue was to be undertaken only by the team of bereavement counsellors. She was worried by my inclusion of healing in my list of interests. I replied that I put it on the form because it is an abiding interest and something which informs my life, but that I would never foist it on anyone. To me it was just a way of being.

That little matter out of the way, I was given a shapeless blue overall, shown around the place and assigned to Frances, a jolly, middle-aged nurse with dyed hair and a face like a knowing barmaid. 'Come in here, dear,' she yelled, yanking back the curtain round someone's bed. 'Do you know how to give a patient a wash?' A poor old man was lying there, naked from the waist down, with a catheter attached to his penis. 'This is George, he's just had an enema and he's making rather a mess,' said Frances wiping his bottom with a J-cloth. No matter how far gone he may have been, I felt it was very unfeeling to subject him to such a humiliating introduction to a new person – particularly a woman.

I took his hand and introduced myself, saying that I'd come to try and help him be more comfortable. He was very stiff and tender and we had to roll him over a bit to change his bed linen. He winced and cried out. 'Whoopsadaisy! There's a good lad,' said Frances patronizingly. Once she called him John by mistake and he corrected her in a barely audible voice, so he was obviously aware of everything that was being said. Frances was very efficient and well-meaning and certainly very friendly to me, but she had dehumanized the patient. He was no longer a man. When I thought of my father or my husband being called 'Lad' or 'Ducky' my blood ran cold.

I was thankful for those weeks I had just spent at the Middlesex. They had given me a model, an achievable standard of excellence against which to measure everything else.

The emotional needs of someone who is ill are inseparable from their physical needs. The whole person – indeed the whole family – is the patient. I had thought a hospice, at least, would hold to these ideals. But ideals are only as good as the people to whom they are entrusted.

In the months that followed I was to see the nursing staff get it right far more often than they got it wrong. That first encounter, though, with insensitive nursing is engraved on my mind and was a timely warning that I should always be mindful of the consequences of anything I might say or do, and ask myself constantly, 'What would I want if this was me?'

'Do you know how to do mouth care?' asked Frances. I said I'd try if she would explain. 'Put on these plastic gloves and take his false teeth out,' she said. Poor George looked at me like a hunted fox. I explained gently what I wanted to do for him and his eyes softened. He helped me remove his dentures and I scrubbed them for him at the sink. The plastic gloves seemed a bit insulting and not really necessary. I massaged some cream into his feet and combed his hair, talking to him softly all the while. I felt miserable and inadequate. He spoke only once, in a weak whisper, to ask for a drink of water and for me to put his hands inside the covers. Then he slept.

During the course of the morning Frances gave me the run-down. Many of the patients, she said, are very negative. They feel that a hospice is a dustbin and see no reason to 'keep on pretending'. They can be touchy and paranoid when visitors – especially nosy volunteers, she added pointedly – seem to be trying to get them to talk. I said I'd bear that in mind, of course. Surely sensitivity to patients' needs includes knowing when to leave them in peace. I also recognized that anyone working in this field needed to be clear about their motivation. Missionary zeal, rescue fantasies, saviour mentality and all notions of a superior stance are just not appropriate attitudes and can be quite a menace. The last person I would want to see looming into focus as I breathed my last would be some holy-moly do-gooder.

As a matter of fact a fairly comical situation had developed at the hospice in that as well as me there were a student social worker, two young nurses learning how to care for dying patients and a visiting American psychologist all lurking around the ward trying to look busy and useful. I did see several patients close their eyes and pretend to be asleep! I was glad to be given a humble but practical task to do – washing out the dirty medicine glasses and cutting up lengths of string for tying up the tops of laundry bags.

George was dying of cancer of the bladder. My next visit coincided once again with his bath-time, and I realized how strong a nurse has to be and how important it is to learn correct lifting techniques to avoid back injuries. Even though he was so thin and wasted he was still very heavy to lift as a dead weight, and all his stiffness and soreness made it very easy to hurt him by mistake. He had a terrible ugly sore place on his poor bottom, so he had to be propped with pillows on his side. We cleaned and combed and rolled and heaved. Then, exhausted, he slept.

It made me sad to think that this was all I knew of him, so I went away and read his notes in the office. I discovered that he had been a security guard in his working days and I tried to picture him as he had once been – strong, fit, tall. Later, when he was more awake, I came and sat beside his bed – not saying anything, just being there, holding his hand and sending him healing. I was very conscious of the mutual nature of the relationship in spite of his extremely weakened condition. We both had something to give and something to learn.

George smiled wanly. 'I've been married since 1936,' he said, and then he slept. He seemed to slip further and further away, drifting into unconsciousness. His family was called: his wife, his sister, his two big burly sons from the building trade. They took it in turns to sit round his bed. I sat with his wife, talking quietly over his apparently comatose body. I told her that thoughts of his long life with her had been the last happy memory on his mind and that he surely knew she was there holding his hand. At that moment his all but lifeless fingers gave hers a tiny flutter and she cried and laid her head on his chest. Then she started to talk about how he used to be in his younger days, and her face relaxed for a while as she remembered him, tall and dark and athletic; won medals for ballroom dancing – natty dresser – looked lovely in his tuxedo . . .

And now here he lay on an incontinence pad, and this was maybe his last day in his poor old body, hands locked with arthritis, no strength, no teeth. Where had the ballroom dancer gone?

His death, later that night, was very undramatic, almost casual, like leaves falling off a tree. He just abandoned his body and was gone.

2

Since I am coming to that Holy Room
Where with thy Quire of saints for evermore
I shall be made thy music; As I come
I tune the instrument here at the door
And what I must do then think here before.

JOHN DONNE

The need to see the living person inside the dying body rather than the dying person was to become an increasingly important theme for me throughout this exploration. At the outset, I was very confused about the concept of the continuing life of the soul. I've never been a religious believer and rather mistrusted what I felt to be a lot of wishful thinking.

'A healthy sceptic' is how I would have described myself. You die and you rot and that's that. Like a cat or a tree, you become nothing more than fertilizer, and the only part of you that continues is the genetic legacy passed down to your children. I'm now beginning to suspect that this attitude masks a great rigidity of mind, a fear of acknowledging and having to surrender to the unknown.

Sitting beside someone as they die has given me a very different understanding. As the physiological sequence of death begins to take hold and the machinery runs down, it becomes apparent that something is leaving, moving into another realm. Something similar to a birth is happening; the spirit that animates the body is taking flight. The body may be old, mentally confused, brain-damaged, falling apart, but the essential being that is taking its leave is ageless and whole and goes when it is ready to go.

I once saw a remarkable piece of film in which a dragonfly larva, an unattractive, brown, papery insect which had been living and growing on the bottom of a pond for two or three years, crawled out of the water and attached itself to a reed. A gradually widening split appeared along its head and back, and slowly, in all its delicate breathtaking perfection, the dragonfly emerged. Tired and weak from its exertions it rested, clinging on to the dry discarded husk of its former self while it gathered strength and its new body was suffused with life. The limp wisps of soggy toilet paper hanging by its side slowly opened and stiffened into dazzling lace wings, and it skimmed away into the evening sun.

Death feels like that. A living process. A continuation, not an ending. The process of abandoning the body doesn't seem to have anything to do with the destruction of the being – it is only a transition, a surrender into other experiences that will pass in turn: '. . . to die into the present moment.' The enemy is not death itself – rather it is the fear of change.

When I was doing Christie Longaker's course I heard for the first time about the ancient Tibetan Buddhist concept of *p'howa* (pronounced po'a), the transference of consciousness at the moment of death. I was beginning to feel that the secret of having a good death might be to cooperate, in much the same way as I learned to do in giving birth. Then I was taught to prepare my mind and body for the event to come. I practised helpful breathing and relaxation techniques for riding the waves of fear, tension and pain. I went into labour alert and aware, with no drugs to fog the clarity and the miracle of the moment. I wanted to be fully conscious and present at the births of my babies, and I want to meet my death in the same way – as a consenting adult, surrendering into whatever comes next. I thought maybe the *p'howa* practice would show me how to effect this ecstatic transition, so when I received notification of a rare visit to the UK by a Tibetan Buddhist master who would be teaching this specific practice to interested Westerners on a remote farm in the middle of Wales, I sent off my deposit immediately.

Maenddlywd is about as near to the middle of Wales as it is possible to be. The River Wye rises on one side of the

33

mountain and the River Severn on the other. It is set in beautiful green rolling farmland filled with sheep and low-hanging rain clouds – an unlikely place to encounter a Tibetan lama. My rickety old car just made it up a rutted muddy track that seemed to be a stream at times, and I arrived in the farmyard to see the incongruous figure of the owner of the house – the 'guest master' as he introduced himself – standing on the front step in a long Zen dressing-gown and Wellington boots, surveying the approach road with a pair of binoculars.

The advertised 'dormitory accommodation' turned out to be a choice between sleeping in a dark, draughty barn on bales of straw, or a windowless firetrap of a loft, or a two-person tent containing three people, with the attendant miseries of sheep shit, soaking-wet grass and no hot water. Not a very auspicious start. I chose the tent, but as I had only a useless pocket torch, I wasn't really properly equipped for camping.

On top of that, neither the Rinpoche (precious one), nor the cook (even more precious one) had arrived. We had been invited to arrive in time for a seven o'clock dinner, but there was a long confidence-depleting wait during which I seriously considered asking for my money back and going home. Eventually a car containing both the cook and the Rinpoche came screeching up the drive and we all lined up to bow a welcome while the guest master lit a special aromatic fire and incense. I felt decidedly bolshie.

But everything changed magically once Chagdud Tulku Rinpoche stepped inside the old stone farmhouse – a beautiful old man from the roof of the world. He stood clad in maroon robes, with a long wispy grey beard and his hair in a topknot. The wide, smooth forehead, the far-seeing eyes with short brows and prominent eyelids, the serene expression and creased laughter lines; something identifies all wise old men, Tibetan, Jew or Red Indian, as a universal brotherhood of tribal elders. What collective noun could describe them? A sagacity of elders?

He had brought with him Jane, his wife and translator, a

34

young American woman who spirited him away upstairs to rest. When we finally ate it was a wonderful, first-class vegetarian meal, infinitely wholesome, but from the kitchen came the unmistakable smell of boiled mutton. 'It's not your imagination,' said the cook. 'Rinpoche eats nothing but meat. He comes from Eastern Tibet where there are no fruits or vegetables so he never eats them.' First surprise!

We received an opening blessing upstairs in the little shrine room before retiring to bed; we were to convene again the following morning at seven for meditation. I didn't sleep well. The tent was on a slight slope and I kept rolling sideways on to the wall of the tent, where the sheep came and peed like Niagara Falls against the canvas. One of the women snored. I didn't think I'd slept at all, but then I realized I must have been dreaming because there was no nice man in my tent when I woke up! The deprivation was getting to me already. No sex, no alcohol and no angry thoughts, said Rinpoche.

The first day was very hard for a headstrong, undisciplined Westerner such as myself. We began with one hour's sitting meditation and chanting. This makes a powerful magical sound rather like a vocal didgeridoo. An invocation to Guru Padmasambhava, the holy man who first passed down these teachings, it has a very hypnotic effect, full of the characteristic chug-chug sounds of the Tibetan language and, I suppose, pitched at the vibrational frequencies associated with altered brain-wave patterns, enabling you to cross more easily into the receptive and spacious part of your mind.

After breakfast we had another half-hour's silent meditation, an hour's teaching and an hour's work (scything the grass, chopping vegetables or mending the tiles on the roof), all for the most part in mindful silence. Then a further hour of teaching, lunch, more teaching, another work period (I escaped and went for a walk), another one and a half hours' teaching and, after supper, a final, optional hour of silent meditation.

Rinpoche spoke a very difficult pidgin English – Jane translated admirably, but we really had to concentrate. She

35

has dedicated her life to being his mouthpiece, has an excellent grasp of the teachings and makes quite difficult concepts almost understandable, but it would be hard for anyone with no previous acquaintance with Buddhist ideas to make much sense of any of it.

Rinpoche was keen to impress upon us right from the start the paramount importance of establishing the proper motivation. It's useless to approach the teaching from an egocentric viewpoint. You could do your practice for sixteen hours a day and not progress one jot towards enlightenment. Westerners, in particular, are always in a hurry, always impatient for results. We want to have all the fun of pulling the ripcord without bothering to learn how to pack the parachute.

The idea is to try to rid yourself of all negativity, to recognize the impermanence of all things, to dedicate your actions to the benefit of all other sentient beings and to learn true compassion in order to improve your karma and thus avoid a rebirth into one of the lower realms.

We are born alone and we die alone, he said; the only thing we take with us across the line of death is our karma – the sum total of our actions and our thoughts. And it is this which determines what will happen next, where we will next be born.

I had learned a bit about karma before, so I understood it better this time. It is not a cosmic balance sheet on which you are awarded pluses and minuses by celestial scorekeepers. It is a very fine and delicate concept of personal responsibility. Negative karma is the result of angry thoughts, cruelty and greed. If you have killed out of anger, for example, the 'hell realm' in which you might find yourself is not literally a place – it is the reflection of your own mind.

'There is no need to ask a psychic or a lama where you will go in your rebirth,' said Rinpoche. 'You have the knowledge within you; you sow what you will reap.' If, in your lifetime, he said, you have acted out of selfish desire, you become a 'hungry ghost', doomed to endless suffering. You will acquire everything you want but be unable to enjoy it. If you act out of ignorance, you will be reborn as an animal – with no free will to make choices. At this point in the discussion the local farmer drove hundreds of bleating, panicking sheep through the farmyard, perfectly illustrating the point right outside the window! In the lower realms there is no freedom to find happiness. Good actions based on bad motives such as envy, jealousy or pride may result in a good rebirth but it won't last. You will become a demi-god, a titan, doomed to a life of unquenchable thirst for power coupled with strife and no rest.

The blissful ideal – to become a Buddha or a Boddhisatva, to be reborn in the 'Pure Land' and achieve enlightenment, the only lasting happiness – is likewise attained through a person's wisdom and clarity. All of us have the essential Buddha nature, but at the same time we have the potential for ignorance, non-recognition and obscuration.

Rinpoche emphasized that all these teachings are symbolic representations for what cannot ultimately be conveyed in words. The 'nature of mind' which we are trying to get to grips with is nothing substantial. It has no shape, form or size. It is

> unbreakable
> unstoppable
> invincible
> indivisible
> indestructible
> truthful
> unchangeable.

You can't say it's there or not there, being or not being, because both are true and not true. Like the Judaic concept of Yahveh, it is unnameable (my father's elderly Jewish cousin always ends her letters 'May G'd bless you'). We have to be able to live with this paradox, to 'rest in the nature of mind'. The Tibetan word for mind also means 'the awakened warrior' – he who would give his life for others.

Given that metaphors are only ever an attempt to translate abstract concepts into recognizable pictures, the main point

37

seems to be that this earthly life is a rare chance to exercise the gift of choice and clean up your karmic act. It is a time to banish obscurity, to confront the nature of absolute truth. Rinpoche gave us this cryptic Buddhist definition of absolute truth: 'If in a dream someone gives us a bag of gold, we are happy. Then if someone beats us up and takes it, we are unhappy. But when we wake up we realize that nothing has been given and nothing taken. This is the nature of absolute truth, but we are caught in the vicissitudes of dreams.'

Suffering or samsara, he said, is a product of our minds' poison, and heaven or nirvana is the product of our own joy. Maturity is to be able to take responsibility for both these states.

What I loved about his teaching, and what makes it so different from most religious dogma, is that we are trusted with the knowledge that the illustrations and the fairy stories are not the gospel truth. They are only 'the finger that points at the moon'. All the symbols and metaphors are to help you uncover the truth – but when you reach it, it is beyond words or concepts. Real understanding cannot be trapped by language.

Rinpoche used wonderful parables and graphic images. An ambitious student, for example, impatient for enlightenment, followed the Buddha's teaching. He read a hundred volumes, went into retreat, meditated day and night for three years hoping for a vision – but there was nothing. He saw only a man rubbing an iron pillar with a piece of silk to make a needle. He meditated for another three years, but all he saw was a man cutting a mountain with a feather. He became very discouraged but meditated for another three years, and saw an injured dog covered with maggots. Moved to tears and not wanting to kill the maggots, he licked off each one. And now the Buddha appeared to him, reproaching him for taking all those years. 'I was each of those figures.'

The man finally understood that no matter how hard you try or how long you meditate, you won't get anywhere without true compassion. It is the key to enlightenment. One moment of true compassion neutralizes aeons of bad karma. The wish to alleviate suffering for all beings is compassion. The wish to create happiness for them in both temporary and permanent ways is love.

Just before one teaching session Rinpoche was beaming and looking out of the window, enjoying the sight of the dogs rounding up the sheep in the farmyard. One way, he suggested, to feel compassion was to recognize all beings as your mother. In one past life or another, *all* have been our kind mothers and all have suffered. With this recognition, he said, you gain equanimity to hold you steady even in the face of extreme provocation. We are all joined to each other. He who attacks you has forgotten his tie to you – he is a victim of his own previous karma. 'Angry not benefit own, not benefit others,' he said in his marvellous English. 'One crazy man jumps cliff – you this example take, not smart!'

The practice of *p'howa* is a way to gain insight, to learn how to direct future rebirths. The alternative for most beings, said Rinpoche, is to be blown powerlessly by the winds of karma back into the cycles of samsara.

'Life's most awesome event is death. Death is inevitable and comes to all without regard for wealth, beauty, intelligence or fame – but *how* you die – terrified and confused or peacefully and with spiritual mastery – is within your control.' The great benefit of *p'howa* is that the signs of accomplishment come quickly without years of strict meditation practice (do I see lots of Western ears pricking up?). Having reached this point you can meet death with confidence.

The main principle is to invoke the desired state by visualizing yourself as a being of light with a central channel opening in a thousand-petalled lotus at the top of your head. This is the path by which your consciousness will travel to the Pure Land and merge with the heart and mind of Buddha Amitabha. It is important to recognize that the traveller, the path and the destination are all aspects of oneself.

'Could a Christian visualize the image of Christ if it was more appropriate?' asked someone. 'If a dying person has

39

practised another spiritual tradition and has a different wisdom being, it's not skilful to introduce a new image,' answered Rinpoche. 'The enlightened essence of Amitabha is like the sky. Wisdom is boundless. There is no division between the wisdom beings. Doesn't matter who makes the vehicle; anyone can use it so long as it is mechanically sound. Tibetans can fly in Western aeroplanes! This vehicle, although made in Tibet, can be used by Westerners to journey to enlightenment.'

The great human foolishness and number one obscuration; we were told, is 'dualism' – seeing ourselves as separate from the whole. Now I began to see the pain of leaving and of loss in a much wider context. Instead of clinging on to how things might have been, we could try to let go of all the protective self-control that keeps us in the prison of our separateness. So at the beginning of each practice session we made a commitment to use our energies for the benefit of others and to dissolve into oneness. The 'self' must risk total dissolution before it can lay claim to the vital energy that will be its core. To be nothing is to be everything.

It seemed to me that this is a perfect preparation for living one's life as well as facing the inevitability of one's death – to meet each moment as it comes with acceptance and compassion instead of fear. This is not passive resignation, giving up or weakness, which is how I've heard some critics describe it. Rather it is an active surrender, a vital courageous stance, the result of an openness and trust in the ultimate perfection of the universe. In effect it is saying 'Yes' to life.

'Like a rented house, your body is impermanent. You don't know when you're going to be kicked out,' said Rinpoche. 'A wise tenant checks out the possibilities of where he could move on to.'

I think by this time we were all ready for the next step. 'Allow your mind to relax,' said Rinpoche. 'Dissolve your thoughts. Instantly you are transformed into the transparent light body.' The central wisdom channel runs through the line of the chakras (the ancient Tantric system of energy centres in the body, along the axis of the spine). Beginning with the lowest, he told us, they are the base or 'secret' chakra, which is to do with union and bliss, the abdomen for inner heat, the heart for clear light, the throat for dreams, and the crown for the transfer of consciousness. These are all doorways, and each chakra has a special practice to open it. At the moment of death, however, we close off all the doors but the highest.

Your clear central channel enlarges slightly, like the bump on a piece of bamboo,at the site of the heart chakra where there sits a white, eight-petalled lotus with a 'green wind' or shimmering radiance round it. Resting on it is your consciousness in the form of a perfectly round drop like a pearl. This represents your fundamental being, your very essence, and when it is time for you to die, it will be propelled up the central channel out of the crown of your head into the Pure Land.

We practised trying to get a clear image of this and did some preliminary exercises, moving the tiny drop of consciousness up and down the central channel like a ping-ping ball on a water spout, limbering up, clearing blockages, making ourselves ready.

I was being conscientious but found it hard to banish unworthy irreverent thoughts of Popeye trying to impress Olive Oyl with one of those test-your-strength machines at the fair where he hits a platform with a giant mallet and a block flies up and rings a bell. Tibetan seekers in their Himalayan kingdom would not have this handicap. Shame on me.

Before attempting the real thing, we had to be initiated into the practice. This is an ancient empowerment ritual passed down directly from one generation of lamas to the next. The whole occasion was quite thrilling, summoning up for me deep reservoirs of collective belonging.

Rinpoche draped his huge maroon and white shawl around himself and put on his magnificent brocade hat. From a little silver jug he poured a trickle of saffron-scented water into our cupped palms so that we could rinse and cleanse our mouths.

41

We were each given a handful of rice grains from a copper plate, an offering to the universe, to throw into the air.

Rinpoche beat on a little drum made from a skull and banded with coral and silver. He rang his brass bells, bringing the magic within reach, calling up the blessing. We chanted prayers once again that we should recognize the suffering of others, that all beings should attain enlightenment; we made a commitment not to harm anything. We chanted invocations, affirmations, intentions, purifications. We sat very relaxed, holding our bodies straight, and visualized above our heads the ruby-red translucent form of the Buddha Amitabha holding a lapis lazuli begging bowl filled with the nectar of life. A shaft of white light poured down from his forehead into our opened channels to help us make the connection. Tantric Buddhism is a feast for the senses. Incense, gestures, music, taste, sound, light; all the perceptions are engaged, leaving very little room for the ego.

'Praying is not about asking; it's about listening,' said Rinpoche. 'It is just opening your eyes to see what was there all along.' Our higher wisdom is not 'out there', it's within us, and only our delusions keep us from recognizing it. In fact only our own cock-eyed concepts create boundaries between inner and outer in the first place.

It was important, Rinpoche explained, to understand all the symbolism. The Buddha sits on a lotus with a sun disc and a moon disc. The lotus represents purity and emptiness, like the womb which gives rise to all creation. From this emptiness comes forth the sun – the female energy of wisdom – and the moon – the male energy of compassion. Just as the male and female energies come together to create life, so in the lotus the sun and moon come together to give birth to the body of the deity. I was very excited by this idea. The birth imagery was so close to the intuitions I had had as I sat with people at the moment of death. The shooting seed of consciousness, the channel, the lotus womb, the blending of male and female – *we are giving birth to ourselves*. Letting go, you die into the present moment – death brings rebirth.

42

I was feeling very high at the end of the day and physically exhausted. I felt as though I had been fishing in the Sargasso Sea, trying to catch the slippery eels of unnameable truths. It had been extraordinarily tiring to sit for such long stretches of time with no back support. The rest periods were too short to take in exercise and sleep; you needed both, and it was dreadful to have to choose.

Ours was a very contemplative and private gathering. Only once did I have a brief glimpse into some dark interiors. Rinpoche was answering questions about ways to do *p'howa* for someone who has been dead for a while, and my tent companion Renata began to weep silently. Her body shook uncontrollably and her face was contorted with terrible grief. I put a hand on her arm to comfort her, and she opened the little book she was cradling in her lap to show me a photograph of her dead baby. She had come here for him. One elderly man who always sat at the back on a chair had nursed his wife at home through her final illness; another had watched his beautiful girlfriend die of cancer. We were all there for our own quiet reasons.

Although primarily a spiritual practice to use for oneself, it is also possible to do *p'howa* for other people. In fact this is a way to put the practice to very good use. It makes you feel better as well as bestowing possible benefits on whoever you're trying to help. It certainly can't do any harm. For someone who is dying, you project your visualization on to them as if you were doing the practice in the mirror, wishing them well – silently if the environment is hostile – praying that their fear be dissolved, holding them in focus. It needs nothing but intention. 'Your attachment to the dying person is good if it is loving and caring,' said Rinpoche. 'It is only not helpful if you allow your emotions to get in the way and you try to hold the person back. Think of the dying person's consciousness being dissolved into light and becoming one with the Buddha or Christ.'

In the case of a person on heavy pain-killing medication you will need to do the practice for them – they may no longer

43

be able to rally their mental faculties. In the case of a person who has already died, there is a ceremony you can perform if you feel there is unfinished business to complete. Take a little food and tea to make an offering. Throw this on the fire or cast it to the winds and, through the power of prayer, imagine it transformed from the ordinary to the extraordinary, to the completely satisfying, so that any symbolic 'hunger' or 'thirst' the dead person may be suffering will be assuaged, and whatever they need will come to them.

It is a beautiful way to say goodbye, to help someone on their way and to dedicate an act of healing to their memory.

'Outside is space, the infinite; inside is mind, the eternal. Transfer of consciousness is the recognition that the two are inseparable.'

We spent all of the following day doing 'the practice' – both the *p'howa* and an accompanying 'long life' practice to fortify our good health and extend our awareness of the daily deaths we undergo. I wasn't very good at the visualizations, but felt a great benefit from doing the chanting and trying to hold the images in my mind. The concentration and stillness, the experience of emptiness, were better than I'd ever managed to achieve before.

I'd never really understood the concept of emptiness before. We are afraid of our own spaciousness because it makes us feel insubstantial, so we keep trying to fill it with things. But like the womb it is the space out of which form arises.

I would never have believed I could sit still for so long and actually enjoy it. The spaciousness seemed to unfold around me and I felt very lucky to be the recipient of such riches. The day ended in riotous eruptions of hilarity. Doing the chores, people kept collapsing into fits of giggles and gales of helpless laughter as tensions were released and normal earthly intercourse was restored. Jokes about the beans for lunch making our *p'howa* come out the wrong end were in marked contrast to our exalted aspirations but reassuringly human all the same.

On the final morning I found myself so full of energy that I rose before dawn, wrapped myself up in my Kashmiri shawl, and sat on the ground outside my tent to watch the sun come up over the green Welsh valleys. I felt more alive than I'd ever felt, and this was after having put into practice, somewhat nervously, Rinpoche's recommendation to think about dying every night.

Some people were worried that the practice could be dangerous and the ejected consciousness fail to return. Rinpoche reassured them that this couldn't possibly happen. 'During lifetime karmic wind is holding body and soul together. Only when the signs of imminent death are upon you does the consciousness separate and shoot off,' he said. 'Once you have the bow and arrow you can shoot it at any time.' I loved his Rabelaisian illustration of the benefits of regular practice: 'Bird fly shitting – not focus, only sometimes rock hitting. Only one-time experience!' Then with an abrupt change of metaphor he assured us that although at first it would seem as if we were trudging on snow shoes, later it would feel as if we were skiing downhill.

'No matter what practice you do, loving compassion is the most important part,' Rinpoche had said in his summing-up. 'Meditation won't work at all without that.' Loving and accepting a person exactly as they are is the only thing you can really do for them.

'Be aware of impermanence, because life is short and everything we do counts. Family relationships and friendships are precious beyond measure. If only we could live our life as if each moment were our last – opening and accepting the as-it-is-ness, the nature of reality – we would connect with that essential part of ourselves that does not die. Ask yourself, is my life equipping me for my death? Because you become what you practise. What you are is what you have been. What you will be is what you are now.'

I couldn't help feeling a little sad that it was all ending, dissolving behind me as I drove away, another small death in the unfolding of my life. But I knew that even as it vanished, as with all things that end, you never really lose them. You carry them with you in your heart and mind.

3

Truth is within ourselves . . .
                . . . and to know
Rather consists in opening out a way
Whence the imprisoned splendour may escape . . .

ROBERT BROWNING

I returned to the hospice and to the stark fact of some empty beds. Ambrose, the retired Jamaican postman whom I'd watched becoming weaker and weaker over my last few visits, had died in the early hours of the morning. His body hadn't yet been seen by his family so it had been placed in the small annexe room. He had been a sweet and gentle old man and I wanted to see him one last time. I went into the room and closed the door. There he lay, eyes closed, face beautiful in its calm serenity. I stroked his cheek. 'Go well, old man,' I said. 'Goodbye and God bless you.' I didn't feel he had completely left the room yet.

I recalled that same sense of presence when I saw my own father just after he had died. He seemed still to be hovering there before taking his leave. To comfort the living? To check out their reactions to his death? Not quite sure where to go? (He was always vague at train stations and airports.) I could hold him, kiss him and tell him I loved him. But when I took my mother to see him two days later at the hospital morgue for a final farewell, he was absolutely gone. Only his chrysalis remained – a lifeless shell, tight and cold. It was so much easier to let him go having seen that with my own eyes.

A bereavement without a body is much harder to bear. Not long ago I got a call from Marie, a thin, anxious woman whom I know slightly because she serves behind the counter at one of my local shops. She had heard I was writing a book about death and asked if I would like to hear her story. She had lost her only daughter in a road accident. After the fatal crash, the parents were called to the mortuary to identify the body. Her husband insisted that he should do it while she waited outside. She wanted to hold her daughter in her arms but was told firmly by the police, who agreed with her husband, that this was a very bad idea. The injuries were extensive. She would only 'upset herself more'. Being half paralysed with shock she dumbly aquiesced and didn't argue. This was six years ago. She had never been able to complete her grief and was still tormented daily by her visions of what those injuries might have been. She was obsessed with remorse. 'How could I have been so weak? How could I not have held my own child? What sight could have been worse than this agony of not knowing? If she had been alive, no matter how horrific her injuries, I would have rushed to her, cradled her, comforted her. Why did her being dead make any difference? How could I have let him talk me out of it?'

The marriage had long since disintegrated. Marie had never talked to anyone and there had never been a day when she didn't think she saw her daughter in a crowd or dream about her calling out for help. The whole story was a nightmare. I was tremendously moved by her desire to share her experience in the hope that it would be helpful to others. I felt that having broken the silence at last, she was longing to move on. I recommended a sympathetic psychotherapist with grief-coun- selling experience and I know Marie has made a lot of progress – not least in being able to give away her daughter's things and redecorate her bedroom.

I telephoned her when I returned from Wales to pass on what I had found stimulating. It's never too late, Rinpoche had said. Prayers are very helpful to a loved person who has died. Your connection with him or her is very strong. After a bad death experience where there has been much suffering and unresolved grief, you can meditate upon the person, call him into the forefront of your conscious mind and visualize his transformation into a body of light. You can talk it through and exorcize the pain. 'Don't waste your difficulties,' was another piece of wisdom from Rinpoche. 'See them as an opportunity, a karmic broom. People can heal themselves with love and compassion. Peace comes with the acceptance of death and with the acceptance and forgiveness of yourself.'

I believe that emotional pain, if it is not discharged, becomes stored in the very tissues of the body. Grief is *work*. If it is not attended to it will surface sooner or later of its own accord, in the form of mental or physical illness. Stephen Levine in *Who Dies?* suggests that it is never too late to communicate love and finish business, even when the loved person is long-since dead. 'It is work that is independent of results,' he writes. 'Done for its own sake. You can speak from the heart and communicate what you still feel separates you. Forgiveness comes when the holding mind sinks into the spacious heart and dissolves.'

Marie asked me to come over to her house. Together we made a little shrine with candles and a photograph of her beloved daughter Lindy. We sat and thought of her, picturing her whole and well and happy. Marie said Psalm 23 and I read a passage from *When Bad Things Happen to Good People* by Harold Kushner, a very helpful book that Dame Cicely Saunders had recommended to me:

> Let me suggest that the bad things that happen in our lives do not have a meaning when they happen to us. They do not happen for any good reason which would cause us to accept them willingly. But we can give them a meaning. We can redeem these tragedies from senselessness by imposing meaning on them. The question we should be asking is not, 'Why did this happen to me? What did I do to deserve this?' That really is an unanswerable, pointless question. A better question would be, 'Now that this has happened, what am I going to do about it?' ... We need to get over the questions that focus on the past and the pain ... and ask instead the question which opens doors onto the future.

The facts of life and death are neutral. We, by our responses, give suffering either a positive or a negative meaning. Illness, accidents, human tragedies kill people. But they do not necessarily kill life or faith. If the death and suffering of someone we love makes us bitter, cynical, incapable of happiness, *we* turn the person who died into one of the 'devil's martyrs'. If suffering and death in someone close to us brings us to explore the limits of our capacity for strength, love and cheerfulness, if it leads us to discover sources of consolation we never knew before, then *we* make the person into a witness for the affirmation of life rather than its rejection.

Marie played 'Sheep may safely Graze' and I finished our remembrance ceremony with the words from Edith Sitwell's poem 'Eurydice':

> Love is not changed by Death,
> And nothing is lost and all in the
> end is harvest.

She cried and I held her and much healing was done that day.

The issue of finding a way to discharge emotion came up again in connection with the death of Ambrose. Mary, one of the staff nurses, had become particularly fond of him and was very upset by his death. One of her duties was to accompany the newly bereaved relatives in to see the body. This is inevitably a distressing time, but she herself had no outlet for her feelings. It would seem to be important that anyone working with terminally ill patients should have access to a strong support structure and regular counselling if they want it. No one can function alone around dying people indefinitely. Nursing, and to a lesser extent volunteer work, is emotionally demanding. All of your patients die despite your efforts, and grieving family members turn to you for support.

The hospices are well aware of this need but haven't as yet

come up with a good solution. Many's the time, said Mary, that she just has to go out and walk in the park with tears streaming down her face. No use telling her husband when she gets home because he doesn't want to know. He has enough problems of his own.

I've heard medical staff say that you just have to learn to be detached, to keep your distance, not to get involved. The trouble with that attitude is that the best doctors and nurses are the ones who do get close to their patients. Involvement and caring are the very essence of healing. Detachment is a fearful attitude, a deliberate psychic numbing to avoid the danger of feeling: afraid to love because you are afraid to lose; afraid to live because you are afraid to die. As someone once put it, 'refusing the loan (of life, of joy) so as not to have to pay back the debt (of death, of sadness).' Defensive psychological structures are built up to ward off pain and stress, but ultimately they ward off life, intimacy and understanding. It's all right to feel; you just need somewhere to discharge those feelings.

Bernie Siegal writes in his inspirational book *Love, Medicine, and Miracles*:

> I became aware that . . . I, too, had adopted this standard defence against pain and failure. Because I was hurting, I withdrew when patients needed me most . . . The so-called detached concern we're taught is an absurdity. Instead we need to be taught a rational concern which allows the expression of feelings without impairing the ability to make decisions.

So he moved his desk against the wall and faced his patients as equals – he committed the physician's cardinal sin and 'got involved':

> By allowing myself to feel as sharply as I could the same pain and fear that my patients felt, I came to realize that there is an aspect of medicine more important than all the technical procedures. I learned that I had much more than surgery to offer and that my help could even extend

51

to the dying and their survivors. In fact I concluded that the *only* real reason to stay in this business was to offer people a friendship they can feel just when they need it most.

Obviously the best way for a doctor to cope when patients are not going to get well is to treat them as individuals of unique worth for whom only one's best efforts are good enough. What a person needs as he faces death is no different from what he needs in life – love, care and sincerity, and to be able to give as well as to receive. A staff nurse from a children's cancer ward said to me once, 'I can't begin to tell you how much strength I get from my patients. Often it is the dying child who is giving strength to all those around him. I remember once a little girl dying of cancer was going to be moved to a private room so that her death would not upset the three other children on the ward. "Please let her stay with us," said the others. "We'll take care of her. We don't want her to be lonely or frightened. Besides, we make each other laugh."'

It seems to me that caring for someone else who is going to die has all the elements of grief, helplessness, failure and sorrow which we so often associate with the process of dying ourselves. Trying to ignore those feelings implies also rejecting them in others, the dying person and the people close to him or her, which can lead to an attitude of callousness. The biggest barrier to providing emotional support is the them/us distinction: we, the professionals, you, the patients; we, the purveyors, you the consumers.

I asked Theresa round to dinner so I could ask her how those who work with the dying cope with their feelings when those people die. Theresa is one of the most skilful and gifted nurses I have met. In fact I have learned more from watching her in action than from any other single source. She is a gentle, calm young woman with an open easy manner and a loving heart.

Whenever she is on duty there is a different atmosphere on the ward. 'The number one necessity is to trust and love the other people you work with,' said Theresa. 'The official support structure here is not really adequate – in fact it's non-existent – but if you know how to ask for it, you can get a lot of help from each other. Those times when you think, "Oh I wish I could tell someone how awful I feel inside," you really need to get it off your chest. "Yes, all right, so you don't know all the answers just because you're a nurse, but you're doing your best," you need to hear. The other nurses, the volunteers and the chaplaincy team make all the difference. They can give you a hug, cheer you up, know when you're sad.'

Theresa comes from a large, close, loving family where there was never any money but always plenty of hugging. I have often seen her stroking a patient's cheek or brushing his hair, joking with him, holding someone's back when they're being sick, washing someone's feet. Little things of incalculable importance. Little things a mother does for a sick child. Little things that make 'non-involvement' an absurdity.

'I've noticed that the nurses who are happy in their lives outside are revitalized when they come back on duty,' she says. 'They cope well and give a lot when they're here but they are also realistic. You can't do it all, you can't take the whole world on your shoulders, so you allow yourself to cut off when you go out of the gate. The ones who find it terribly stressful are the ones who don't have a good environment to go home to. Nothing gets discharged. They can't cut off. They can't admit their own weaknesses. They can't say when they're feeling inadequate or sad, so they tend to become totally task-oriented.'

I have watched this syndrome in action too. There is one stone-faced nurse with loud heels who bangs through her jobs and gets everything done efficiently but casts her eyes heavenward in an expression of extreme martyrdom every time a patient rings a buzzer (which seems to happen much more frequently when she is on duty, in the atmosphere of tension that she generates). I'm sure she has no malicious intent but,

53

for whatever reason, she is a miserable old bag and infects everyone around her with disquiet. I once even saw her take someone's buzzer and deliberately put it out of reach because she was annoyed at being summoned so frequently. The old lady, it has to be said, *was* being very demanding, but now she became quite frantic. There had to be a better way of dealing with her.

It seems to me that the whole point of hospice care is that it should allow time for loving encounters. Meaning is so often found in the humdrum, the endlessly repetitive and insignificant. As nurses or volunteers we can help dying people feel valued and dignified in the way we give them the gestures of personal contact – not just drips, tubes and infusions.

Theresa will often sit at someone's bedside for an hour, holding a hand, talking, if that's what the person needs most, or just being there. The bed-making or the bath can wait. Watching her, two lines from T. S. Eliot's *Four Quartets* came to mind:

> A condition of complete simplicity
> Costing not less than everything.

Sharing Trudi Bird's last days gave me an opportunity to put some of these thoughts into practice.

Trudi Bird was eighty-six years old, a Hungarian lady who'd been in England for fifty years and lived up to her name; she had beady bright eyes and lots of sticking-out white hair which gave the impression of tufty feathers. I warmed to her immediately. She was so anxious when she first arrived that the doctor feared for her heart. I mentioned that her skin looked a little dry from having been in bed and asked if she would like me to give her a gentle facial with some sweet-smelling aromatherapy oil. She smiled her assent.

When I first came to the hospice I began very tentatively to use some of the techniques of healing in situations where cure was not a realistic objective. This attempt gathered momentum as I gained confidence and formulated my ideas. Massages and facials for example can accomplish a lot in the way of relaxation and relief from tension and anxiety.

The words 'healing', 'therapy' or 'treatment', which might

54

be rather threatening, don't ever need to be mentioned. It is wonderful to see how the beneficial effects of warm physical human contact begin to work almost immediately. The sick person's breathing becomes less rapid and shallow; blood pressure becomes lower and heart-rate slower. There is instant relief from dry flaky skin, poor circulation and bed sores. Aching bones and muscles feel better; swelling is reduced. The input of loving energy makes people feel less lonely, frightened or isolated. A massage stimulates easy conversation and is a great reliever of boredom. Relatives are reassured to see that their loved ones are being personally cherished over and above good nursing care, and often feel encouraged to try it themselves, which multiplies all the good effects tenfold and gives them something useful and positive to do.

If it seems appropriate I talk about the concept of visualization, harnessing the mind's extraordinary image-making capacity to help create a relaxing scenario and make oneself feel better. Many elderly people, especialy if they live alone, have not been touched in a loving or sensuous way for years and years. I personally believe that this physical deprivation is the root cause of much ill-health in the first place and a problem which our society hasn't even begun to tackle. There is one further small but important point to note. To give a foot massage, for example, I always sit on a stool lower than the patient's chair or bed. Instead of having yet something else done to him from above, he can then retain, symbolically, a measure of dignity and control.

The increased feeling of well-being and relaxation resulting from a gentle massage has the effect of reducing pain and therefore, possibly, the person may have less need for strong medication. People feel relief from headaches, constipation, indigestion, insomnia and breathlessness.

All this is in addition to the beneficial and curative properties of the essential oils themselves – geranium, lavender, orange-blossom or camomile.

That first little face massage forged a wonderful relationship between Trudi Bird and me . . . I sat with her a lot, took her to the toilet and so forth, and she reminisced about Budapest. She was thrilled to hear that my father had spoken with a 'funny Continental accent' like hers. She was dying for a proper sausage, she said, cackling conspiratorially, but would make do with a saveloy if it were possible! I said I'd smuggle one in for her. She was terrified of making a fuss or seeming to complain and lay sweating with heat rather than ask for a fan. 'Thank you, good lady,' she said over and over again when I got her one.

She was a widow with no children, her only visitor a guilt-ridden, worried, overweight nephew who had recently suffered a stroke himself and rushed backwards and forwards between his aged mother (Trudi's only sister), who was in a home, and Trudi. She kept telling him not to bother, that she didn't want to be a burden and so on, but actually conveyed quite a different message and made him feel even more guilty. The games families play are very complex and impossible for an outsider to unravel. Being drawn into taking sides would be fatal. The only useful stance is an even-handed, non-judgemental one.

One morning when I asked Trudi how she was feeling she answered, 'Smiling on the outside, crying on the inside.' She spent a lot of time fretting about what was happening to her and what would become of her flat with her not there to keep an eye on it. With one breath she expressed paranoid fears about her pension book, saying she thought her nephew was trying to cheat her, and with the next she castigated herself for all the 'wickedness' and 'selfishness' of her life. Everything came tumbling out in a jumble. 'Why won't the doctor tell me how long I have to stay here?' she asked. 'When can I go home?' Then, 'I'm frightened of suffering. Don't let me suffer.' And a few minutes later, 'I'd rather have the pain than take any more tablets. Oh, dear God, You can take me up now! I'm ready to go.' She held tightly to my hand and cast her eyes to heaven as if she expected instant lift-off.

She wanted to talk to the doctor and wanted me to stay with her so she would remember all the things she had to ask him. She told him she felt worse in the morning, couldn't sleep at night, had to get up to pee six times nightly, was afraid she'd wet the bed, couldn't see, eyesight failing, everything breaking down ... 'Thank you, sir, for listening to an old duck,' she said when she'd got it all off her chest. I don't think she expected much. She just needed to tell him and for him to sit there and listen.

At one point she said to me with big tears in her eyes, 'Please go away – when I see your smiling face it makes it so much harder to leave this world.' A moment later she asked me if I would be with her when she died. 'Of course,' I answered. I massaged her thin feet and she slept.

The next time I saw her she was refusing all medication including painkillers and refusing food. She just wanted to die as quickly as possible and kept on asking the doctor to give her 'something to speed it up a bit'. She begged me for some ice when she saw me. I gave her some iced water to drink, then held an ice cube in my hand to make it cold before holding her wrists and stroking her brow. She gradually went off to sleep and slept all morning. As I watched her lying there, I marvelled at the tenacity of the life force. Every beat of her heart, every breath unwilling, and yet ... If I could have willed her to die then I would have done. I don't condone euthanasia; although Trudi kept hinting at it, I never felt she really wanted to go through with it. What she was seeking were reassurances that she would not be in pain or left alone.

Two days later she was serene but much weaker – hardly there at all. She seemed to have worked out all the conflicting emotions that were making her fret. She had gone through what seemed to be a preparatory grief about her own death and reached the fabled 'acceptance' stage I had read about but never seen before.

Lovely nurse Bridie came to cleanse Trudi's mouth for her. It was dry and cracked, with a horribly coated tongue. Bridie took a little gauze swab held in a pair of plastic forceps and gently cleaned and wiped Trudi's mouth with a mouthwash, then put glycerine on her lips. 'I feel so sorry for anyone with

57

such a dry mouth,' Bridie said in her soft Irish brogue. 'It must be really miserable and uncomfortable.' These little skilful kindnesses make all the difference. Trudi smiled faintly, signalling her relief.

I brought ice again to cool her and she whispered, 'Oh how lovely.' I could hardly hear her, she was so far away, but every so often she'd say 'I want to go quick' or 'So lovely to sleep' or 'Goodbye'. She said goodbye quite a few times and held my hand, and smiled a beatific toothless smile that creased up all her laughter lines.

Trudi looked peaceful and radiant, and coped without any obliterating drugs. I realized it wouldn't matter who was there at the precise moment of her death because she was dying all the time. It was like watching the lights go out one by one on a big ocean liner. The only discomfort she had was a sore spot on her bottom which had developed because she didn't like lying on her side. We lifted her on to a soft sheepskin to relieve the pressure points on her body. She had by this time been catheterized, so she had no need to worry about wetting the bed, and since she wasn't eating, her bowels were not a problem.

I didn't think I'd see her alive again. I kissed her, willing her to die, and left a message with the office asking them to ring me if she asked for me. Theresa rang at midnight to say she'd died peacefully and happily just then. I felt a sharp pang at the thought of those little beady eyes dimmed for ever but I was very grateful for such an encouraging demonstration of how to die well.

One day I asked Theresa what she says if a patient asks her about the hereafter. 'I just say I don't know. I don't feel called upon to come up with any spiritual answers,' she said. Sometimes not knowing can be the wisest state. Most of us underrate the capacity of the human heart. We think we can only be useful by knowing something, but often not knowing and just being there allows us to be simply available to someone else. Stephen Levine's books emphasize this point again and again. They gave me heart and encouraged me to understand that even in my helplessness I can be useful, even in my uselessness I can be helpful.

We can provide no answer to what happens after death, no guarantee of a heaven, a sublime afterlife, or a hell for that matter. Again I asked myself, what would I want? I would trust a person who said 'I don't know'. In fact, said Theresa, very few dying patients want to talk about it much. They do not expect answers or miracles. 'What they ask for are assurances that they won't die alone or in pain and that I *can* promise. People are more afraid of being alone than anything, and many worry about whether you're still going to give them that tender, loving care after they've gone. "Please be kind to me after I've died," they'll say. Or "Will you be the one to wash me? See my relatives? Take my body downstairs?"'

Most hospitals still use the old tin trolleys. A porter comes along and chucks the dead body on to one like a piece of meat. 'Stiffs', they're called, and they're bundled about with total lack of respect. Rattle, bang. 'I think our hospice is very good at handling death with dignity,' Theresa said, 'at allowing time and space. We tidy a person up a bit and leave her looking peaceful with a single flower on the pillow beside her head. Her relatives can sit with her for as long as they like. There's no hurry.'

While I had been away in Wales, several new patients had arrived on our ward. Their contrasting family situations were so crucial in contributing to the quality of their final days that I began to think a lot about context and relationships. No one dies in a vacuum. You bring your entire history with you.

Enid was very ill when she was brought in. She'd had a bad day the day before I met her, so her eighty-two-year-old husband Tom had stayed the night, sleeping upright in a chair. The poor old man was distraught and sat weeping by her bed. 'Oh God!' he kept choking. 'What will I do without

59

her?' Sixty-two years they'd been married and they had three middle-aged daughters, but various family stalemates were hindering communication. 'Oh dear me, ain't it awful,' said poor Enid, without her teeth, in total bewilderment, over and over again.

Bereavement seems hardest of all when it hits the old who are very frail and helpless. They've often lost many of their friends and relatives already and are overburdened with loss. Tom was inconsolable in his shock and panic, fear and worry. He wouldn't go home or eat anything so the staff made him as comfortable as they could and made it possible for the couple to be together all the time. (In one hospice I know of there is a private room with a double bed for just such occasions. It should be a standard feature.)

Enid was moved to the single room to allow for a little more privacy. On her last day she was barely with us, but Tom refused to leave her side. He just wept piteously and held on to her hand for dear life. I got him to talk a bit about his memories, and it seemed to be doing him good. The 'old days', when things were happy and different, if only in his imagination, brought him a brief respite from his sorrows.

Just then one of his daughters, a hard-faced woman in her late fifties, arrived in response to a telephone call from Theresa. She had her meek-looking husband in tow; he did not say a single word during their visit. The woman glowered accusingly at Theresa, almost as if to say, 'You got me to come all the way here telling me she was dying – what's she still alive for?' I left the room tactfully but I could still hear her having a go at the old man: 'I do my best! What do you expect? It costs a lot of money to get here. I couldn't come any sooner. What more do you want me to do? It's not my fault . . .'

Theresa thought it might be a good idea to have a private talk with her and asked me to sit in on it to give her moral support. She asked the daughter what was troubling her and what kind of support the old man would be able to depend on once his wife had died. 'Well, we can't have him!' the woman

snapped, adding defensively, 'We haven't got a spare room.'
There were, it seemed, a younger sister ('always my mother's
favourite') and an older sister ('always my father's favourite').
Tom had expressed a wish to go and stay in the north of
England with the youngest, who ran a hotel and had a caravan
and a couple of horses. Old Tom had been a horse-and-cart
driver for a brewery company in his working days, and
thought he could live in the caravan and help with the horses
to earn his keep.

The daughter in question had driven down from Yorkshire
– she drove down and back in one day, a round trip of nearly
500 miles – and arrived at the hospice at 3 a.m. She'd had a
quick kip in the day room, didn't want to see her mother ('for
fear it would upset her'), told her dad he wouldn't be able to
come to her, and left after half an hour. The eldest daughter
hadn't visited at all. Ill-health was her reason.

As the middle daughter talked, all the poison of a lifetime
seeped into the room like a pool of pus. 'He was a hard man,
my dad,' she said, 'very hard on me. Never showed his
emotions.' And there he sat in the next room, a helpless,
frightened, broken old man. Could it really be the same
person? Later, when she was standing alone in the corridor
looking bad-tempered and impatient, I said to her, 'I'm so
sorry. It must be dreadful for you to see your Mum like this.'
She nodded and looked into the distance. 'Were you close to
her?' 'A lot closer than what she was to me,' she answered
bitterly and then quite suddenly burst into tears. 'I don't
think she ever loved me,' she sobbed. 'Certainly never stood
up for me against him, the vicious old bugger, with his
crocodile tears.' She jerked her thumb in the directon of the
room where Tom was sitting with his head in his hands. 'I
don't feel anything for him.' I put an arm round her shoulders
and she cried softly for a few minutes, then shook me off, blew
her nose loudly and walked off down the corridor. How much
sadder it must be to lose parents you don't love than ones you
do.

She never came back. Enid died that night and I heard

later that Tom returned to their little flat where he steadfastly resisted all the efforts of the Social Services to move him into an old folks' home and died within a month.

Annie was only fifty-six but looked like a much older woman. She had once weighed fourteen stone but now weighed four. Thin as a broomstick, she'd had a double mastectomy and now had secondary tumours in her spine. She smoked one cigarette after another, stubbing them out on a wet tissue. As a non-smoker from the time my mother died of smoking-related emphysema, I found it hard to sit with her and endure such a disgusting habit – too many painful memories of Mum's awful wheezing, her hacking cough and her nicotine-stained bedroom ceiling came back to me. Apart from that, Annie was lovely to be with: a woman of magical sweetness who made everyone want to do things for her. She loved to talk and told me how much she had always enjoyed cooking, especially baking. How there had been a home-made cake on the table for tea every day and how she'd made her niece's four-tier wedding cake and a photograph of it had appeared in a bridal magazine.

Very weak but with a contented look on her pretty face, she basked in the devoted and constant care of her large loving family. Her bedside table was crowded with flowers and photographs of smiling children. One of her daughters stayed till eleven every night to give her a final wash before sleeping,and creamed her skin all over so she wouldn't get bed sores. The family calmly and confidently did everything for her and my only job was to get comforting cups of tea for the relatives and to keep them company, chatting about anything they wanted to talk about – children mostly, or Annie and what a terrific mother and grandmother she was. As soon as the hospice had got her pain under control, they gathered her up and took her home to die in her own bed.

* * *

Poor muddled Constance, a big fat woman, was there one morning when I arrived, and I was asked to help her have a bath. She was very confused and agitated and kept muttering about a key she couldn't get in the lock. The doctors suspected a brain tumour and were doing tests. Her dear gentle husband, Wilf, came every day to take her out in the garden. At seventy-four he was wonderfully fit; ex-Irish Guards, ramrod straight, with a neat moustache. 'This isn't her,' he said briskly, recalling his vivacious bride of fifty-two years ago. 'The drugs have made her like this.' I suggested that maybe a little massage might make her feel calmer and less anxious. She looked worried but Wilf persuaded her to try it, so after lunch I gave her legs and feet a very gentle massage and she loved it. Once again I felt glad to have developed the confidence to offer this; most people respond so favourably. It was also tremendously useful to learn some of the basic nursing techniques needed to care for very ill people: how to wash and feed them, make beds as they lie in them, help them to sit on a commode. It is important not to be afraid; just to be there whatever happens, never forgetting the person inside the dying body.

Over the next two weeks Constance lay on her bed like a walrus. Her growing brain tumour made her speech very difficult to follow and jumbled her thoughts. You had to strain to pick out the relevant words like 'pee pee' or 'water'. It must have been a terrible frustration for her. Once in the middle of the slurred ramblings I distinctly heard 'I'm trying.' 'I know you're trying, Constance,' I said. 'I'm so sorry I can't understand everything you're saying. It's not your fault.'

She sat out in a chair and ate her lunch by herself, getting mashed potato down her nightie and ice-cream in her cavernous cleavage. Then she wiped her face with the warm flannel I gave her and collapsed on to the bed like a small mountain. My intuition was that if I was to find her at all it would have to be in the distant past – not in this wretched present.

'You're the only one who takes any interest in me,' said Constance to me one day – crystal clear and completely out of the blue, while I was massaging her feet and humming to myself. She'd never spoken to me directly before and I was startled but delighted by this further evidence that heart-to-heart communication works. In the few moments of clarity that followed she held tightly to my hand and I sang 'If You Were The Only Girl In The World' to her. I don't know why I chose that; I just remember loving my Mum singing it to me. 'There would be such wonderful things to do. I would say such wonderful things to you,' she joined in, and fragments of memory like torn clouds drifted across the horizon – smoke signals from the other side of the hill.

It was to be her birthday at the weekend. Wilf, encouraged by her improved condition, decided to take her home for a family party, but it wasn't really a success – she became terribly exhausted and more confused than ever. When the ambulance brought her back the following Monday I was quite shocked to see how poorly she looked. She just slept and slept, so I sat with Wilf to keep him company. All day he was on the verge of cracking but his military training held him together. He wouldn't show his feelings. Every time I created an opportunity for him to do so, he'd change the subject, get up to water a dry-looking plant, or turn on the television. He blew his nose a lot and polished his glasses. He had tears in his eyes but he would have died rather than let them escape.

Suddenly Constance took a turn for the worse. 'Wilf, Wilf, I'm dying,' she said. 'Now don't talk like that,' he cried, visibly distressed and choked up. He just couldn't bear to hear the words. 'You're going to be fine, just fine.' But her heart was packing up. Her arms went blue, then white, then freezing cold, then clammy. She couldn't get her breath. The doctor gave her a tranquillizer and two shots of morphine. She calmed down but slipped out of range. Wilf held her hand helplessly, blaming himself for having taken her out at the weekend. With his other hand he fished in his breast pocket and brought out a photograph of Constance taken a few years before: a good-looking, jaunty woman wearing a cossack hat on a winter holiday.

We sat together for the next few hours and watched her struggle to leave her body. It struck me once again how like a birth death is. But the main problem here seemed to be the atmosphere of denial. Constance had known all along she was dying. I feel sure she was ready to die. She'd seen her family and had her birthday party and her heart had decided to stop; it seemed a much better option than waiting for the brain tumour to kill her slowly. But with no preparation and no guidelines it was all very messy; she gasped and laboured and Wilf pretended it wasn't happening. I think she was waiting for *permission* but all she was getting was a 'Don't die!' message and heavy medication. I would hate that.

All I could do was just be there. I didn't know how to help Wilf in his buttoned-up despair. I didn't have the confidence to say, 'Just tell her you love her and that it's all right for her to go.' I remained worried and puzzled about the problems of pain, anxiety and drug use. Sogyal Rinpoche – a leading Tibetan teacher in the art of dying – recommends the cessation, or at least the reduction, of pain-relieving medication twenty-four hours before death in order to allow more clarity and control for the last acts that need to be performed and for the disembarkation of the soul. And how can you tell when death is twenty-four hours away?

I talked to the hospice matron, to senior nursing sisters and to a doctor about this dilemma and about the challenge of humane and holistic pain management. Everyone's needs are different, I was told, and many patients require nothing at the end. It depends upon the nature of the illness and the individual's resources. If over many years, a person has become accustomed to using painkillers and tranquillizers for every least little thing, this is not the time to re-educate them. Hospices don't always get it right, they freely acknowledge, but it seems better to err on the side of too much pain relief than to give too little. The important thing is to respond sensitively to individual wishes, and certainly not to impose your own theories about how someone should work with pain.

I guess that conscious dying has to evolve from conscious living. What I personally have to be careful of is the temptation to want other people to die my ideal death for me. In truth there is nothing to sell, no philosophy to push. All you can give another person in the process of dying is the love and the space to do it their own way. There is no 'best way to die'.

Another new patient was Molly, a cartoon hag with wild straggly hair. On her bedside table she had a toy black cat stuck full of pins, a Cornish pixie sitting on a rock, and a deck of tarot cards. She was eccentric, demanding and cantankerous. 'Quite a character!' said Theresa. 'Quite a pong!' said blunt Frances, making little effort to disguise her distaste. Both nurses had been shocked by the condition of the dressing that covered her suppurating ulcer when she was sent over from another hospital. 'Disgusting! Call themselves nurses? Look at the state of this!'

Molly was obviously upset and disorientated, showing her feelings by throwing her weight around. She didn't want sheets – 'too namby-pamby'; she liked sleeping in blankets. She shouted as Theresa and I tried to make her bed. Theresa teased her a bit but it wasn't the right approach. 'Oh God!' groaned Molly in despair and misery, putting her head in her hands.

It must be unbearable to feel impotent when you have been a matriarch – tyrant, even, the eighty-two-year-old head of the family, and suddenly young whipper-snappers the age of your grandchildren are telling you how to make a bed. I tried to tidy her hair but she didn't like that either and twisted it into two ratty pigtails. So I held her hands and said, 'Is there anything I can do to make you happy?'

'Oh Lord, don't be nice to me,' she croaked, bursting into tears, 'you'll only make me cry.' But she held on to me with her bony fingers, big tears plopping down, and I told her I was so sorry everyone seemed to be bullying her but we just

66

wanted to make her comfortable and no wonder she felt cross. Next time a nurse came into the room Molly said, 'Sorry, dear.'

In the afternoon her daughter Lil arrived, an enormous humorous woman of about sixty with a wet cigarette stuck to her lip and one eye permanently screwed shut against the coil of smoke. She looked like one of those gypsy women who accost you in Oxford Street with a sprig of lucky heather. She blew into the nurses' office, without knocking, while we were relaxing with a cup of coffee. 'Thought there's a few things you ought to know about the old girl,' she said, leaning against the doorframe. 'First of all she hides her food. You think she's eating but she stuffs it down the bed. Last week we found half a dozen fucking sausages in there.' It was such a hilarious image that I found it hard to keep a straight face. 'Second, I want a social worker down here to sort out her pension. Someone's been cashing it and we don't know what's happened to the effing money. Third she's a gruff old cow but she's brought up ten kids and never done no harm to no one.' Her chin jutted forward and her voice cracked. The belligerence was a poignantly thin disguise for her feelings of protectiveness and love for the dying old battle-axe.

From then on the whole noisy, volatile, unconventional clan of Molly's family traipsed in and out day and night. Lil proved herself the most loyal and loving daughter, trudging over on the bus with great-grandchildren in pushchairs to see her every day. The babies played happily on the old woman's bed, ate her fruit and stuck pins in her cat. On the days when Molly felt a bit better she gave everybody hell. She chucked her tea on the floor and once threw her stuffed cat across the room at poor genteel Mary, the patient in the bed opposite, who was promptly sick from the shock of it all. Her family laughed at her affectionately, teased her and indulged her, while allowing her to flap her feathers and put up a show of power and influence. But most of the time she was uncharacteristically subdued – almost as if she couldn't believe that her roaring great Irish temper was not going to keep death at bay.

67

One morning when I called in to see her I was told that she'd been very ill in the night, coughing up blood. She looked scared and fragile, so I sat with her and massaged her feet. I was glad to see she'd been allowed to sleep just in her blankets. Lil was upset to see the old dragon with the fighting spirit gone out of her, but deep down she accepted the inevitable and didn't try to hold her back. From this time until she died forty-eight hours later, Molly's mood was completely different. She stopped eating, stopped hurling things about and having a go at people. She lay with her moth-eaten little black witch's cat tucked in her arms, occasionally opening her eyes and smiling. In her own way, she had made her peace and come to terms with dying. The Roman Catholic priest came to give her a last blessing and she literally gave up the ghost there and then.

The will plays a fascinating part in determining the actual moment of death. I talked to one of the doctors about this. He said that after all his years of experience he was still no better at predicting it – each individual seems to have his or her own inner clock. A person will often wait for a particular event such as the birth of a grandchild, an eightieth birthday or the arrival of a family member from abroad, and then let go.

Watching Molly's rumbustious, chaotic family deal with her dying was a good lesson for me. I saw clearly that if a dying person seems angry and hard to get along with, he might well be angry not with you but with the attributes you represent – vitality, freedom, strength, self-determination – which he has lost or is rapidly losing.

One morning we had a new admission brought in while I was there – a dreadful looking sight. Poor Vernon, sedated to a stupor, was breathing in rasping gasps. His parched mouth was shiny and dry like a charred salamander's, locked open in a silent cry. Sitting beside him was his common-law wife Ada and her teenage son. As soon as I came into the room she started talking at me in shock and relief. She told me how she had tried to look after him at home – he was much older than she – for as long as she could, along with his 102-year-old ungrateful bloodsucking bat of a mother and his 47-year-old mentally retarded sister . . .

She was at breaking point, and Vernon, terrified that Ada would be taken from him, became violent every time she left the room even to go to the lavatory. He was also fed up with the three-hourly painkilling injections which were administered by a home-care nurse, and had kept on trying to get out of bed and escape from the house. I said I'd sit with her until the doctor arrived to fix up the morphine pump; this would deliver a constant measured dose to keep the pain level down and obviate the need for disturbing him with more injections. Ada talked non-stop. I knew the only way I could help was by being an available space.

Vernon made a semi-conscious mime of attempting to put something in his mouth. 'Oh look,' said Ada, amused. 'He wants his pipe, bless him.' She jammed it between his teeth like a baby's bottle and he sucked on it weakly. Vernon was dying of cancer of the bronchial tubes. His breath smelled vile and his tongue was stained bright yellow.

Eventually the pump did the trick and the atmosphere of panic subsided. Poor Ada was greatly reassured by the care and efficiency she witnessed and no longer felt so guilty about not being able to keep Vernon at home. When he eventually died she said, 'I watched the agony and despair go away. His face went back to how he was when I first met him. I've never seen anyone dead before but it's beautiful.'

Their predicament clearly demonstrated to me that the desirability of dying at home depends crucially on what the home situation is like and how much help and support the carer has. The load Ada had been carrying was unendurable. Her escalating crisis had got out of hand and she had no resources left. When my friend Tina's sister was dying of cancer at the age of forty, the strain on her at home, where she thought she wanted to be, was just too much. Home was where she was in charge, and she had to keep on organizing

things even though she was dying. 'Have we got any marma-
lade?' her husband would yell up the stairs, or 'How do you
make gravy?' She couldn't relax for a minute and found that
she was supporting everyone else in the family because they
were all falling apart without her. Moving to the hospice for
the final weeks was a blessed relief – there were no more
everyday responsibilities to preoccupy her and she had the
reassurance of round-the-clock nursing. They got her pain
down to 'a bearable level', as she called it, enabling her to
enjoy what was left of her life and feel in control of her dying.

Another old man was brought in the same day as Vernon.
He'd been found living alone in abject squalor – filthy clothes;
a bucket of urine and vomit in the middle of the floor; dirty
cups; burned pans; old food; spit and phlegm everywhere. The
ambulance men had to break the door down and cover their
faces with handkerchiefs in order to go in and get him. Two of
the nurses gave him a bath, and when I saw him he was
sitting in a chair wearing little green knitted footwarmers and
stripy pyjamas. He looked rather bewildered and was wheezing mightily from his lung cancer. He had been extremely
resistant to being spruced up. As Molly's had been, his entire
identity was threatened just at the time when he was most
vulnerable. I can understand the need to hang on to your
habits and your character even if it is not in your best interests,
and I was impressed by the courage of this frail person; he
had refused to be dominated and depersonalized to the
impotent position of 'patient' – especially 'dying patient'.

It made me think about the question of how one can open
one's heart with someone who is dirty or aggressive or
touching areas of vulnerability in oneself. I came to the
conclusion that it is all right to be ill at ease but very important
to be honest about it. I have never forgotten Elisabeth Kübler-
Ross's dictum that a patient must be allowed to die in
character. The nurses were wonderfully sensitive to the old
man's needs – just accepting him for what he was. He died
the very same day. I'm glad he was wearing warm hand-
knitted slippers and had been rescued in the nick of time from

dying poor and old and alone. '*Abbandonato*,' said the Italian lady in the next room. We were talking about the fate of many English pensioners compared with the rather better deal that '*vecchietti*' – the little old ones – get in Italy. All of which was starkly underlined by the story of Edward . . .

I had been asked, because of a shortage of voluntary drivers, to ferry a patient to hospital for an appointment with his consultant, so I went to collect him and his nurse escort from another ward. Edward was an elderly gent of the old school with a marvellous brown-velvet voice. 'I would really be most awfully grateful', he said with immense charm and panache, 'if you would also kindly drive me to my flat and to my bank as I have some business to attend to.' I agreed, of course, and it turned out that his bank was miles away on the other side of London. What he really wanted was the excuse for a little outing. He asked if it would be possible to drive past the Maids Of Honour tea shop in Kew so that he could treat nurse Kate and me to a cake, so we made the detour. He even wanted to buy us lunch in his pyjamas. We demurred, but there was no stopping him going into the bank to make his transactions in person.

A huge disfiguring tumour covered half Edward's face, making him blind in one eye. There was an unsightly open wound underneath the big dressing he wore on his head. His determination to conduct himself with the utmost dignity and correct old-fashioned manners despite his suffering was very moving. The old man had been a teacher of English, French and German to adult students for thirty years and had published two little books on chess puzzles. He never complained, and was as talkative and cheerful as etiquette would demand and painkillers would allow, sitting in the back of the car with his walking stick.

After his visit to the hospital I drove him up along the Terrace Gardens and through Richmond Park in the beautiful late October sunshine, so that he could feast his one remaining eye on the grazing deer and the autumn colours. He wanted, he said, a last glimpse of such earthly delights to sustain him through the darkness that lay ahead.

We arrived eventually at his flat, and I was shocked to see the conditions he had been living in. He had recently been forced, because of deteriorating health, to move from his home of many years to this so-called 'sheltered housing' – a concrete block of tiny, one-roomed cells under the general supervision of a warden who was linked to all tenants by an alarm bell. Apart from that the residents managed entirely alone and cooked for themselves.

Edward's room was dark, smelly and airless. It contained one ripped leatherette armchair, a broken-down single bed, a squalid little kitchen area and a few pathetic possessions piled in disarray. The floor was covered in a repulsive orange and brown, 'fiesta'-patterned, synthetic-fibre carpet. Oppressive ugliness permeated everything, but he'd still tried to make it look like home. A photograph of himself and all the other organ scholars at Corpus Christi College, Cambridge was stuck on the wall with Sellotape, along with a snapshot of his old friend Gavin Maxwell, a handful of military decorations and a newspaper picture of Karpov cut out of *The Times*. Even in his extreme frailty he had wanted to leave his mark on the soulless place, and he wanted us to see these clues to the life and passions of the man behind the bandage.

Compared to that of some old people his housing was probably considered good, or at least adequate, but our elderly folk ought to have something better than this. An environment so devoid of physical and aesthetic comfort is a bleak one in which to end your days. My heart ached at his dignity and his aloneness. He ferreted about a bit, collected his mail, looked for and couldn't find his green corduroy trousers, salvaged his battered old typewriter, and we drove back.

He was content at the hospice, he said. All the nurses adored him, and his gentle manner and unfailing courtesy created an atmosphere of serenity. His own perception of his lot was that incredible good fortune had brought him to a safe harbour at the end of his life. I sensed in Edward almost a sense of wonder, a willingness to surrender himself to the vast ocean of his being and trust in the ability of the water to hold him up. A couple of days later, he died.

As Stephen Levine says, 'You have to be able to let life be before you can let life go.' He tells the story of one dying cancer patient who said to him, 'My body may be falling apart but I have never been more whole.' It had become difficult for him to speak, but on the day he died, surrounded by his family at home, he indicated that he wanted crayons and a piece of his five-year-old's drawing paper. He drew his family standing outside a house surrounded by trees and flowers and pets; they were holding hands and looking at the sun. At the bottom he wrote a quotation from Crazy Horse, the American Indian shaman: 'Today is a good day to die for all the things of my life are present.'

One of the nurses told me the story of a dying old man she had once nursed. His voice had almost gone from cancer of the throat, but when he spoke it was with a lovely soft musical Irish lilt. One day she said to him, 'You must have had the most glorious singing voice.' 'How did you know?' he whispered. 'I was indeed a beautiful singer.' He proceeded to sing all fourteen verses of an old Celtic lament while she listened spellbound. She didn't realize it then, she said, but he was singing his own death. He never spoke again and a week later he died.

A deaf, senile old lady called Mavis arrived one day. Everybody shouted at her – 'ALL RIGHT DEAR?' or 'HOW ARE WE TODAY?' or 'FEELING COMFY?' – and she just looked out on the world as if from behind a plate-glass panel and nodded her head. Dealing with deafness is a tricky problem. It's very difficult to behave normally towards a person when you are yelling at the top of your lungs. Also, shouting loudly or speaking excessively slowly always seems so insulting. I remembered a good practical suggestion from Elisabeth Kübler-Ross's workshop: a double-sided speaking board. Key phrases, parts of the body, needs and wants are written in bold letters on a piece of card for the patient to point to or nod at. The chart would be useful for anyone with loss of hearing or speech or, if adapted bilingually, for a foreign-language speaker.

Mavis didn't want to eat. She didn't want anything much, but needed to be frequently fed with drinks from a plastic beaker. When I had some spare time, I went and sat by her bed and held her hand. I didn't say anything but just looked at her and smiled – trying in the stillness of the moment to reflect on my own feelings of loss and vulnerability. In all these old ladies I see my own mother lying there and I want to be for them as I would have wished a stranger to be for her – kind; compassionate; seeing the pretty young woman, the lover, the mother, the strengths that have lived and are living still inside the failing shell. I dedicate my ability to be loving and useful to her continued memory. That way her best qualities can live on in me, granting her eternal life.

For a moment I felt overwhelmed with tenderness for the tiny, white-haired, senile little bird woman before me. I stroked her hair and she suddenly looked straight into my eyes and smiled at me, almost conspiratorially. There was an instant of pure communication before the mists swirled in again. This was the first time I experienced for myself something I have since found to be true again and again; that when working with seriously ill people or those in a coma, with very little children, animals or mentally handicapped people – whenever words are not adequate or appropriate or when things are no longer being hidden by words, perhaps – it is possible to communicate silently, heart to heart. Separation melts away and we seem to be united in a common bond. 'Don't just do something, stand there,' a wise Catholic nun said to me once. One of the nurses on the ward said of an old man who had been paralysed by a stroke and couldn't speak, 'It was very easy to have a deep relationship with Cecil. Silence itself is full of meaning if you respect each other.'

This intuitive link, one of the prime ingredients in healing, has become sadly undervalued in Western society although it thrives in many tribal cultures. My husband Richard, who is a documentary film maker, once spent some unanticipated time with a tribe of Amazonian Indians when his helicopter broke down in the Brazilian jungle. Although he and they had no common language, he said it was uncanny how the Indians always intuitively picked up his mood. If he wanted to be on his own they faded out of sight. If he was feeling anxious or melancholy, someone would magically appear at his side, put a hand on his arm, beam at him, try to cheer him up. This faculty is not lost in the West, just lying dormant. We need to resurrect it.

Later that afternoon I was talking to one of the social workers about caring for mentally confused dying people and she told me the story of her own mother, whom she had nursed at home for as long as she could. The old lady had had Alzheimer's disease, pre-senile dementia. She would throw tantrums and was incontinent and abusive, but there were occasional moments of complete lucidity. Her daughter had the intuition that the memory bank, which she likened to a box of colour slides in the mind, had all spilled out on the floor and been stuffed back in random order, giving her mother no control over recall of events or their accompanying emotions.

'How old are you now, Mum?' she would ask in the middle of a violent tantrum. 'Are you three?' Her mother would nod. So long as she allowed her to be a baby and acknowledged what was happening, the whole thing made sense and she coped as well as she knew how. Alas, circumstances made it impossible for her to continue caring for her mother at home. In the psycho-geriatric ward where she eventually had to leave her the nurses shouted and punished her when she dribbled her food, messed the bed and cried like a baby. She eventually died a horrible lonely death trapped in the body of an angry infant.

I know that pre-senile dementia is supposed to be caused by a premature deterioration of the brain, a hardening of the

75

arteries. But in my experience there is nearly always an emotional or symbolic component to an illness. It occurred to me that perhaps there was an unconscious desire here for revenge on an unresolved, unexpressed childhood; for a last chance to retrieve and relive it, to indulge once and for all the sulks, regressions and tantrums denied to a behave-yourself, restricted, *unfair* childhood where the anger never got aired and the shit never got smeared. Could it be that by acknowledging that possibility one could release a person from the need to complete the process? Or is it too late? Has the brain already deteriorated too far?

I just have an intuition that the whole person who is in there somewhere recognizes the truth at some level, and if we the carers see it too we may be able to reach through the confusion and set them free. By tuning into the heart, from that place where we can experience another person within ourselves, we can say without words, 'I hear you, I understand you and I accept you just as you are.'

One old lady in a geriatric ward was unable to speak. After her death, her locker was emptied and this poem was discovered, written on scraps of paper amongst her personal belongings:

Kate

What do you see, nurse,
    What do you see?
Is this what you're thinking,
    looking at me –
A crabbit old woman
    not very wise,
Uncertain of habit
    with faraway eyes,
Who dribbles her food
    and makes no reply,

When you say in a loud voice,
    'I do wish you'd try',
Who seems not to notice
    the things that you do,
And forever is losing
    a stocking or shoe,
Who resisting or not
    lets you do as you will
With bathing or feeding
    the long day to fill,
Is that what you're thinking,
    is that what you see?

Then open your eyes,
    You're not looking at me.
I'll tell you who I am,
    sitting so still
As I follow your bidding,
    eat at your will.
I'm a small child of ten
    with a father and mother,
Brothers and sisters who
    love one another,
A young girl of sixteen
    with wings on her feet,
Dreaming that soon now
    a lover she'll meet:
A bride soon at twenty,
    my heart gives a leap,
Recalling the vows
    that I promised to keep:
At twenty-five now
    I have young of my own
Who need me to build
    a secure happy home.

A young woman of thirty,
    my young now grow fast,

Bound to each other
    with ties that should last:
At forty my young ones
    now grown are soon gone,
But my man stays beside me
    to see I don't mourn.
At fifty once more
    babies play round my knee,
Again we know children,
    my loved one and me.
Dark days are upon me,
    my husband is dead,
I look to the future,
    I shudder with dread,
For my young are all busy
    with young of their own,
And I think of the years
    and the love I have known.
I'm an old woman now
    and nature is cruel,
'Tis her jest now to make
    old age look like a fool

The body it crumbles,
    grace and vigour depart,
There now is a stone
    where I once had a heart;
But inside this old carcass
    a young girl still dwells,
And now and again
    my battered heart swells;
I remember the joys
    I remember the pain,
And I'm loving and living
    life over again.
I think of the years
    all too few – gone too fast,

And accept the stark fact
    that nothing can last.
So open your eyes nurses,
    open and see
Not a crabbit old woman;
    look closer – see ME.

4

Hope is the basic ingredient of all strength. It moves the soul and motivates the will. It is a call from without and an answer from within.

ERIK ERIKSON

Having spent many months at the hospice learning how to care for mostly elderly dying people, I was aware that the issue of death at the end of a long life is very different from its sudden intrusion into the midst of life. And it was at just about this time that AIDS swept into our lives with a furtive ferocity that took everyone by surprise. Suddenly the media were full of it, sensationalizing and spreading panic. Someone we knew in America died of it at the age of thirty-two: the spectre was knocking on the castle gates.

Although we were bombarded with statistics and conflicting information, it seemed clear that with the number of those affected doubling every ten months, AIDS would become the biggest premature killer of them all, running neck and neck with breast cancer, and that within three years it could already be outstripping heart disease, lung cancer and death on the roads in the 20–40 age group. Beyond this, AIDS seemed to have acquired a symbolic, almost biblical significance. 'A fitting disease of our times,' I heard it called; 'divine retribution;' 'an apt punishment for mankind's self-destructive disposition.'

On the other hand, Elisabeth Kübler-Ross was saying that AIDS should be seen as an 'incredible blessing' because it was forcing us to make a choice. 'AIDS poses its own threat to mankind,' she says, 'but unlike war, it is a battle from within, knowing no borders or national boundaries. Are we going to choose hate and discrimination or will we have the courage to choose love and service? We can destroy ourselves with our own self-imposed fears, blame, shame, negativity, we can become very vulnerable to diseases and more panicky when the number of AIDS patients reaches a million or more, or we can make choices based on love and begin to heal . . .'

In the first couple of months after a national phone-in network had been set up to provide advice on AIDS in England, 35,000 people called, 80 per cent of them heterosexuals and 60 per cent of them women. With 3,000,000 people who were HIV antibody positive in the United States alone, it seemed that in a very short time everyone would be personally affected or at least know someone with AIDS.

'Don't Die of Ignorance,' urged the huge posters, but I for one felt quite helplessly ill-informed. The government hand-outs were not particularly helpful; nor were the television campaigns featuring icebergs and tombstones. One day, on the notice board at the hospice, I saw that someone had pinned up a leaflet announcing an introductory course on AIDS counselling organized by the Centre for the Advancement of Counselling. It was open to anyone so I signed up.

Most of the other people on the course were health-care professionals of one sort or another – nurses, social workers, counsellors and therapists – and we all felt that our most pressing common need was for medical information. We wanted to find out what AIDS is and what it isn't, what it does and doesn't do and where the greatest risks lie. Obviously you need to be acquainted with the basic facts in order to be even remotely helpful to someone with the disease.

Those basic facts were very lucidly explained by the tutor in the introductory session. The first surprise for me was to learn that there is no such thing as the 'AIDS virus', an inaccurate and misleading label which conjures up a no-hope situation of terminal illness. Nobody actually dies of AIDS; they die of one of the normally harmless organisms which hang around the body and only become life-threatening when the immune system breaks down.

AIDS is caused by a virus called HIV (human immunode-ficiency virus), which has the sinister ability to copy the structure of the cells it invades – the so-called T4 'helper' cells – one of the crucial groups of white blood cells whose specific job it is to orchestrate the fight against infection and malignancy.

Once a person has contracted the virus it rests quietly in the healthy T4 cells until they are called upon to fight a bug. At this point the virus wakes up and reproduces itself. The host cell is killed and becomes a virus factory, hurling out copies of itself to latch on to other T4 cells, after which it lies dormant again. This can obviously become a terrible down-ward spiral, as every time the replication process is awakened the immune system becomes more and more depleted. Stress and worry further dampen its resources, allowing infection in. The wake-up process is activated more and more frequently until the T4 cells have all been invaded and destroyed. This is the point at which the patient is said to have developed AIDS; the once-powerful defence system can no longer hold the marauders at bay.

Most people with HIV infection feel entirely well and may remain so for years. It's not at all a foregone conclusion that they will get worse, although some may feel ill with swollen lymph glands, rather as if they have glandular fever, at the time they 'seroconvert' (i.e. become HIV antibody positive).

If a series of other symptoms begin to occur, such as massive weight loss, lethargy, fatigue, fevers and drenching night-sweats, explosive diarrhoea, skin problems and oral thrush, these are collectively known as ARC (AIDS-related complex). Patients in this category, tormented by uncertainty and fears of further deterioration, need a lot of help and support. It is now widely believed that psychological factors, including people's vulnerability to stress and anxiety and their ability to manage these, play a crucial role in determining the physical response to infection and the likelihood of someone's develop-ing AIDS from the HIV virus. This also applies to other chronic diseases such as cancer – the power of the mind to influence the course of an illness should never be underestimated.

AIDS if it does develop, usually takes the form of

1) **Opportunistic infections** – common or garden disorders which are now able to run amok and take advantage of the weakened defence system;

2) **Nervous disorders** – which can affect the brain or cause blindness;

3) **Malignant tumours** – such as the unsightly skin cancer, Kaposi's sarcoma.

The next facts to get straight were those of transmission. HIV is a fragile virus easily destroyed outside the human body by very hot water or a 10% bleach solution. It is impossible to catch it by casual contact. Nursing a patient with AIDS is not dangerous unless you're very careless about hygiene. The only way to become infected is for the virus to enter your bloodstream. This can happen via sexual intercourse from man to man, from man to woman, or from woman to man (lesbian sex carries virtually no risk). The type of sexual activity involved is obviously an important factor: rectal intercourse, for example, may cause bleeding.

The virus can be passed on through the sharing of hypodermic needles in intravenous drug use, through transfusion of contaminated blood or blood products, or through the placenta of an HIV-positive mother to her unborn child. Although the virus has occasionally been detected in saliva and tears, it is in such a low concentration that it could not effectively transmit itself. Hugging, kissing on the cheek, shaking hands, sharing cups, cutlery, toilet seats or towels, and comforting someone who is crying are all perfectly safe.

We were given a lot of practical advice about the complicated issue of testing – and counselling people on whether or not to have the antibody test. If it were me and I suspected that I had somehow contracted the virus, I would definitely want to know, in spite of the horrendous implications. Alas, there are many cruel examples of schools, workplaces, hospitals, even church congregations, rejecting or ostracizing a person diagnosed antibody-positive. One doctor refused to treat a woman patient with AIDS, saying, 'She can go and slit her wrists for all I care. I won't have anything to do with her.' On top of everything else, there can be problems with mortgages, insurance, credit cards, hire companies and employers. It is important for people to know what their legal rights are, especially in regard to confidentiality, and what services are available in the event of their having to face the worst. It is also important for them to feel that they still have some measure of control over a life seemingly overtaken by catastrophe.

To be helpful at such a crisis point in someone's life you need to see them not only as a whole person but also as part of a wider constellation of interlocking parts . . . Do they live alone or with friends, family or a sexual partner? Do they have a network of friends or do they feel isolated? To what extent do they rely on sex, perhaps, for social contact? How will their partner take the news? If a person is gay, are they openly gay? Do their family know? Do their friends know? Does almost no one know?

This led to a frank session on safe sex. Since AIDS is mainly a sexually transmitted disease, it's important that people should be able to talk openly about sex without embarrassment, to articulate their needs and fears and to talk to their sexual partners about what's enjoyable, acceptable and safe.

The task of counselling is to give someone an opportunity to explore and clarify his situation and discover ways of living more resourcefully. It is about helping him to view himself from a more constructive viewpoint and to realize that there *are* areas over which he has control and about which he can make decisions.

In order for any of this to be possible, the counsellor has to be able to communicate sympathetically – and that doesn't mean just verbally. So much is conveyed by gesture, by eye contact and other subtleties of body language. Particularly when the issue at hand is a complex or frightening one, it can be quite difficult to break the ice. You don't have to be brilliant at talking and interpreting. You're not there to solve the person's problems for him – the principal skill a good counsellor needs to acquire is that of active listening.

Counselling is a relationship by agreement, a conspiracy of emotional consent, half-way between talking to a friend and psychotherapy. More importantly still, it is about giving back to the other person that which he has lost – confidence, knowledge of what to do, where to turn, awareness of the part he himself is playing in the mess he finds himself in – as well as the chance to be listened to and taken seriously.

The best way to learn this is to practise it, so we did lots of exercises in pairs, taking it in turns to be the 'client', counselling each other on an AIDS-related problem, and then discussing what was helpful and what was alienating in the 'counsellor's' manner.

Everyone felt that it was unhelpful to have opinions or advice imposed on them, forcing them to remain in a dependent, childlike position – almost as bad, in fact, as the opposite extreme of trying to talk to someone who wasn't really interested.

What emerged from all this was that there are three phases to the counselling process. The first is the development of trust; creating a safe place where the person seeking help can unpack his problem and express his feelings at his own pace. Butting in at this stage is not constructive. The person knows more about his problem (and probably about the next step he should take) than you do. All you need to do is be wholly present, staying with the pain, conveying 'Yes, it's OK to talk about it,' and 'Yes, I'm listening.'

The second phase is exploring the options. Here it is helpful if the counsellor can summarize what's been said and tentatively express what's been implied, reflecting back patterns and recognizing themes. This is easy if you've been really listening to the 'music behind the words', as the tutor put it.

Phase three is 'What next?' If changes are necessary, what

85

constructive action can be taken? Here the counsellor can help the 'client' to set a few achievable, realistic goals. Clear thinking, keeping one's feet on the ground, and not being too ambitious were seen as useful attributes in the counsellor at this stage.

By the time we'd all had the opportunity to experience both sides of the counselling relationship, we knew each other a bit better and there was a feeling of safety and confidence in the group. This was just as well, because the next session, 'Looking at Death and Bereavement', became very emotionally charged.

At forty-six years old, I was probably the oldest person there, and working on this book had given me ample time to ponder my own mortality. It is a subject that most people in their teens and twenties postpone, especially in the West. We take life for granted – our obsession with youth and fitness makes personal acquaintance with illness and death much more remote. We tend to associate physical suffering and death with news coverage from the Third World, but AIDS is changing all that and bringing everything into sharp focus.

When we were asked to work with a partner, I paired up with Joey, a pale, tense young man from Scotland working as a nurse in a big London teaching hospital. The question we were to consider was, 'If you had a year to live what difference would it make?'

My thoughts were quite practical and philosophical: I'd try to attend to any unfinished business, do my *p'howa* practice more conscientiously, spend time with the people I loved, talk to them about my hopes and wishes for my own *conscious* death. I'd allow myself the fantasy, if I felt well enough, of travelling to a couple of the places I've always wanted to see – Bali, Peru, Madagascar. Knowing that I had a time limit would give me the incentive to concentrate my mind on the choices that were open to me, forcing me to confront any unresolved conflicts and address a few spiritual matters . . .

Joey looked at me with intense hostility, as if I were a millionaire distributing largess in the slums from my carriage window – or Marie Antoinette playing milkmaids. 'Bullshit!' he said, disregarding everything we'd just learned about the counsellor's neutral role. 'How can you say that?' His eyes narrowed and he sat forward in his chair, his face one inch from mine. 'Try some of these questions instead,' he snarled. 'If you were dying of AIDS, how would you most hate to die? I'll tell you. Dementia. The fucking virus gets in your brain and you lose your marbles. Your personality changes and you become a monster, you don't even know your own lover, you dribble and piss yourself.' His face was contorted and the veins stood out on his neck. 'And how about this one. What terrifies you most about AIDS? Catching it, is the answer. Catching it and dying like he did. And here's another one. If you died who would be glad?' He covered his face with his hands and began to sob. His voice cracked. 'My father would be glad. My God-Almighty-hardnut-bloody policeman father would be glad.'

He looked up at me, his eyes streaming, then quickly looked away again. 'I'm so sorry,' he said. 'I don't know why I said that. All this is nothing to do with you.' But it was. I had triggered off his unexploded bomb and he had chosen to blow up in my face – to confide his deepest feelings of anger, sorrow and fear in me. In my fathomless inadequacy, I knew I had nothing to offer but the space for him to do what he needed to do. He was about the same age as my youngest son – he could have been my son. I reached out and gently stroked the side of his cheek with the back of my hand.

He put his spiky head in my lap, locked his arms tight around my waist and let the tears come. His body shook with great shuddering convulsions, and I remembered my own relentless catharsis wrapped in the blanket, sucking my thumb on the floor of my mother's flat. What I had needed then – what he needed now – was to be a baby, to return to a time before language when the world was all feelings and sounds and smells, to howl like the wind, to abandon myself to the force of the elements and yet know that I would not disintegrate.

I held him and rocked him and he cried for a long time,

retching, gagging, gasping for breath, oblivious to everything else in the room. The class tutor could see that the situation was under control, and when the session broke for lunch everybody else slipped out, leaving the two of us alone. When the tempest had subsided, his head still in my lap and his face turned away from me, he began to speak, his voice hoarse and raw. The words tumbled out so fast that I could barely hear them.

He told of the rapid deterioration and death of his lover from AIDS dementia nine months before. A funeral parlour had refused to handle the body after its staff had ascertained the cause of death. Joey's own father, an evangelical Christian, said it served him right, it was God's punishment, he'd brought it on himself, and as far as he was concerned he no longer had a son. His mother was more loving but afraid to anger her violent, bullying husband, so he didn't see much of her. And now, he'd recently had the test done himself and been told *over the phone* that he was HIV positive.

His pain was so intense, the time ahead of him so bleak, that I felt quite paralysed with the enormity of it all. What would become of him? There would be no magical release, no instant solution. All I could hang on to was my conviction that advice or anodyne words of comfort would not help him. I stroked his hair, giving him only the most extreme attentiveness of which I was capable.

Timid, shy, no good at sport, with a weedy physique, this gentle boy who liked cooking and flowers had felt all his life the weight of his father's disappointment while longing for his love and approval. His father hated 'raving pooftahs' and 'mincing queens' with an irrational rabid fury, and Joey had not told his parents that he was homosexual until his friend was dying. 'You sick bastard!' was his father's response, and the look on his face had been one of pure disgust.

He lay quietly for a while, then sat up abruptly and blew his nose. 'I'm going out to have a cigarette,' he said, and disappeared without another word. He didn't come back for the afternoon workshop and I felt terrible – worried sick that he would do something drastic in his fragile state. Phase one of our impromptu counselling session had been so precipitate that there had been no opportunity for phases two and three, exploring options and setting goals. How rarely does life play by the rules. But there was nothing anyone could do – he was a voluntary participant on the course and had a perfect right to leave before the end if he wanted to. He and I had no relationship to build on, no contract beyond the fact that we had selected each other for that particular session.

My only option was to trust the healing process. I tried to remind myself that life acts of itself – you don't have to interfere, shouldn't limit someone's response by projecting *your* need to see results. The trick is to love enough, unconditionally; not to give it direction, but allow it to travel beneath the surface to where it needs to go. People must make their own discoveries and their own journey. After all, Joey had chosen to come on the course in the first place: he had already begun to seek change.

'Be with others as far as they will allow your strength to take them, enfolding without holding on,' Elisabeth Kübler-Ross once said, 'and fill with your own being the remaining space when they move on.'

I remember some of the wisdom I had learnt from Gaston St Pierre when he taught me the principles of the Metamorphic foot massage technique some years ago: the patient is the seed; the practitioner the earth, the catalyst. He repeatedly stressed the importance of being rather than doing. 'Get out of the way,' he would say. 'Don't impose your own needs or opinions, will or ego.' His philosophy was the ultimate in allowing and letting go – trusting the patient's or recipient's innate intelligence for transformation. 'There is only one expert and that is the life force of the patient.'

But it is hard to believe what you know to be true when you're caught up in a real-life crisis. I felt as if I'd failed somehow – not been able to contain Joey, sustain him, save him. I've had the same awful feeling of impotence often enough with my own children, knowing that with all the will in the world I cannot protect them from pain and that my concern cannot save them from anything.

Later on Andy, one of the other gay men in the group, mentioned that he worked with an organization called London Lighthouse – started less than a year before as a project to build an AIDS hospice offering a loving and supportive environment to people with AIDS and their families. I also learned that it held regular thirteen-week training courses for volunteers and had begun to create a network of neighbour-hood teams all over the metropolis to offer home support, friendship and help to anyone affected by AIDS. Andy had done the volunteers' course and was now so passionately committed to Lighthouse that he had given up his job in order to work there full time.

Andy promised to send me more information and it arrived by post the next day. Within a week I heard that my application for a place on the autumn training course had been accepted. No one should ever have to die like Joey's lover; no one should ever have to feel as isolated as Joey. His name was on the address list of course participants so I wrote telling him about Lighthouse and what I was going to do and how profoundly moved I'd been by his predicament, but I never had an answer.

In each of us rest the innate qualities of a natural goodness and a love of truth. We are all born fine, strong, intelligent, loving, powerful, creative human beings and are fully equipped to help and heal others in need. This is the convic-tion that informs and inspires Lighthouse. The reason that we don't always measure up to our potential is that things that have happened to us in the past get in the way.

In order to be able to 'be there' for someone, especially someone who has AIDS, allowing them to express whatever their feelings are without taking it personally; in order to be able to listen and love without judging, you have to be getting your own needs met or you will be a menace. You have to be up-front about why you want to do this work in the first place and have a forum for dealing with your own distress. So many people with a great desire to be helpful to others use it as a way of diverting attention away from their own despair. This isn't helpful to anyone in the long run.

What is helpful is to be clear of your own rubbish – to learn how to release your own emotional baggage – and for this you need someone to be there for you. Lighthouse had evolved a good system for tackling this – after each teaching session we would subdivide into our own small support groups and 'co-counsel' each other. This allows for a relationship of absolute parity where no one is the expert but everyone has the opportunity to listen and to be heard in equal parts, giving and receiving interested, relaxed, undistracted attention.

We talked about what made us feel bad, what made us feel good; where we thought we'd failed, where we knew we'd been effective. One of the most important points was to be able to boast about where we thought we'd been terrific – in the outside world, that's considered rather bad form, but here you could crow and be stroked. Right from the beginning and all the time volunteers continue to do this work, they stay together as a little family, meeting regularly, being an outlet for one another.

As I write this now, having been part of my group for a year, I know that the eight of us are passionately devoted to each other and that between us we could cope with nearly any crisis of life or death. We couldn't be a more unlikely bunch of friends – in the normal course of events we would probably never even have met, let alone chosen to spend time in each other's company – but our acceptance of one another and commitment to the basic Lighthouse philosophy has forged a tremendous bond between us.

We made up quite a representative cross-section of the British public. Some had lost friends and lovers from AIDs, some were already diagnosed HIV positive, some didn't know what their antibody status was (most of us fall into this last category and just assume we have no cause to worry). We were a balanced group of men and women, young and old, waged and unwaged, heterosexual and homosexual, united by our common desire to do something about AIDS. If we are afraid of AIDS we will not be able to tackle it. Knowing that we can act together as a self-created community and have the power, individually and collectively, to make a difference gives us all a feeling of strength and optimism.

Over the course of the next thirteen weeks we explored many patterns of behaviour and ways of coping that most of us use unconsciously all the time to keep at bay the pain and rejection in our lives, and looked at how these consistently undermine our immune systems, making us vulnerable to infection and ill health.

'AIDS is just a disease, and like all diseases it can be fought,' says Christopher Spence, one of the founders of Lighthouse, in his inspiring book *AIDS: Time to Reclaim Our Power.* 'Conventional medicine is unequal to the task. As a society we have colluded to abdicate our individual responsibility for guarding against our susceptibility to this or any other virus infection, for combating the onset of serious illness that can result and for facing up to the meaning and opportunity of death as its ultimate consequence in some cases. Like nothing else in our time, AIDS has demonstrated that the game has outgrown its own rules and that something radically different is called for.'

A good place to start is to look at the many ways we suppress our immune systems. There are the obvious physical factors such as poor diet, polluted environment, overwork, lack of sleep and exercise, addiction to cigarettes, drugs, alcohol, etc., but the subtle emotional factors – lack of self-esteem, isolation, depression, shame, not being true to yourself, feeling you are a victim – are much more significant. So many of the symptoms that break out through AIDS are inside us all along.

A long list grew on the blackboard as people called out their 'immuno-supportive' suggestions:

Sharing, honesty, acceptance, clear-thinking, humour, plenty of cuddles, good breathing, sunshine, self-respect, joy, creativity, forgiveness ('If you are unable to forgive, there's a place where you will never heal,' said our group leader). These all welcome and enhance the life force. When you have a life-threatening disease, they become crucial.

So what stops us leading a wonderful immuno-supportive lifestyle? Another long list; and the chief culprit was fear. 'If a child is made fearful within itself, it holds back its true emotions,' said someone. If we are not allowed to express our true self, the self we express becomes false and we become hypocrites. Fear, not hate, is the opposite of love. If we cannot feel or express love, we feel fear. We become afraid of life. Unable to love ourselves or even believe we are worth loving, we begin to doubt the very existence of love or happiness, and therefore become subtly self-destructive.

Low expectations, coupled with a deep-seated lack of self-esteem, makes a person into a prime target for anything which is going to attack the immune system. It's very hard to understand the concept of unconditional love if you haven't known it as a child. For most of us as children, love is very conditional: the message is, I'll love you *if* you're a winner, eat your dinner, pass exams, don't upset your mother, fulfil our expectations, be like me. And so we develop survival strategies. In order to be lovable we conform, perform, pretend, try too hard, appease, rebel, manipulate, play people off against each other, play the clown; all in an attempt to make us feel better about ourselves because we've become disconnected from our essential lovableness.

Here in our Lighthouse group we were encouraged to ask ourselves the fundamental questions: Do I live my life in ways consistent with loving myself? What have I done today to myself that I wouldn't do to my best love or to my child? The greatest love of all is to heal the child within ourselves. Only then are we free to recognize and to heal the child within others. What do I really want? What am I doing about it? How can I ask for help and am I willing to receive it?

These are good questions at the best of times. When you are facing AIDS or any other serious illness they become urgent. If you don't love well, death will always come too soon.

These are a few of the people who spoke up in front of the group:

Celia talked about not valuing herself. After her divorce six years ago she has lived alone but for one son with whom she's always having rows. Although she is an extremely caring person, she doesn't care well for herself. She allows herself to be put upon, gets very tired and overwrought, suffers from excruciating migraines and eats for comfort and insulation, so that she has become overweight. She had a beloved friend who developed AIDS – perhaps the only person who ever saw and loved the real her inside – and he had died only a few months before the course began.

Arnie is an intense young man. He operates on a very short fuse and is quick to imagine that people are doing him down. He is extremely bright, but his childhood conditioning has branded him a trouble-maker, too clever by half. He has been unemployed for ages and has a chip on his shoulder as big as the Ritz. Ever since his early teens he has used getting drunk as a means of numbing his frustrations. He has recently discovered that he is infected with the HIV virus and talked about how much he wants to alter his self-destructive life patterns while there is still time. He also knows how good he is at being a listening ear for desperate people who ring up while he's manning the Lighthouse switchboard.

Toni became very tearful as she talked about feeling scared that she wouldn't be adequate for this work. The recent death of a patient with AIDS at the hospital where she works had reopened all the wounds she sustained when her brother died in the same way. Would her feelings of sorrow overwhelm her? she wanted to know. Would she be able both to keep her

94

professional objectivity and work out her own grief in an appropriate way?

Roberta spoke about her need to monitor stress in herself. She is a very private person and finds it most difficult to share anything of herself. She talked about a dying patient she had nursed and felt she hadn't done enough for.

Charlie, who is HIV positive and determined to fight, spoke of the tools he is using – a new commitment to his Christian beliefs and a daily regime of prayer. He talked of the challenge of living and the despair of loveless, promiscuous sex, of being open to the possibility of changing the dead-end behaviour patterns in one's life. He is a lovely, brave man.

I spoke about my tension from trying to carry the world on my shoulders, knowing that I have to learn to stop rescuing people, stop being everyone's Mummy. To ask when I need help and to make time for myself to do the things I know make me feel good – meditation, t'ai-chi, relaxation. I'm always afraid to show my anger and my weakness. What if people won't like me? ('Horrid.' 'Aggressive.' 'Undermining.') What if I don't live up to their expectations? ('Not as great as she's always trying to make out.' 'Thought you could rely on her.') What if they find me out? ('She's only five years old inside that middle-aged body.' 'She's not a real writer at all. She's only Allegra.')

John, a drug-user for many years, spoke about the difficulty of making an investment in real life. You become engulfed by futility, he said. The size of your problem seems to fill all the available space, your motivation drains away and a mood of apathy descends. He was asked to come forward to participate in a demonstration.

One of the beliefs of Lighthouse is that we live in a society which is hellbent on making addicts out of people. From smoking to shopping, from alcohol to casual sex, we don't discharge our pain – we find ways to numb it. Our need for comfort, love, self-confidence is never met, and so we compulsively search for something which will fill the empty space. The issue of sexual addiction – 'cruising' – is an important one in the context of AIDS. Telling people about safer sex isn't enough. In spite of all the information you might be given, if you feel isolated, lonely, worthless, you won't be able to stop. To break an addiction you have to feel you're worth it.

People who are addicted are, of course, lovable, the same child they always were. Whatever they have done is the best they could do at the time with the resources they had. John was encouraged to remember back to the time when drugs first became his friend. How did it make him feel? What was it like? Standing up in front of everybody he told the story of how he was taken away from his foster mother whom he loved and given back to his real mother who hated him and punished him whatever he did. He became paralysed; unable to act for fear of doing the wrong thing and getting belted.

As he reached his teens he had no confidence, and his only courage – a sense of bravado and camaraderie – came from the drugs he was introduced to by some older kids. Obviously to tell a person like John to give up his habit because it's bad for his health and might even kill him is meaningless. It has too many associations and is, in fact, an old friend. It will only be possible for him to let it go when he can replace it with something he wants more.

One of the facts I've realized when trying to teach people ways to take better care of themselves is that often they really don't want to. They constantly sabotage themselves because what they really want is for someone else to take care of them. So much ill health is the result of a deep desire to escape from responsibility. The child inside needs nourishment, so the way forward begins with the tackling of unmet needs.

Everyone was very moved by John's courage in exposing his innermost secrets, and he received a lot of love and support in return. In a situation like this nobody will divulge more than they want to, and we all have our own answers inside us. We just need to find a safe place to leave our old baggage of emotional hurts. A place where we will be listened to with loving and undivided attention. A place where we can cry if we want to or scream or rage and where we won't be interrupted, humiliated or ridiculed.

What I found so impressive here at Lighthouse was the basic assumption that we could all learn to make such a place for each other, that everyone has the innate ability to help someone in need – to be a good listener, to be a good friend.

Your very vulnerability makes you even more valuable. You don't need qualifications or letters after your name; you don't need to be an 'expert'. For our part, we were just a bunch of ordinary human beings united by the desire to do something about the problem of AIDS. We all knew that none of us were going to be able to stop the AIDS epidemic single-handed but we were convinced that we could create a feeling of community and safety so strong that no one need ever experience despair or isolation again.

One night I wrote in my diary: 'I hope that during this course I will come to understand homosexuality better. For someone who likes to think of herself as enlightened, tolerant, accepting, I don't understand the phenomenon properly at all. How much is physiological? How much rebellion? How much self-destructive? How much a search for love? Is it glandular, psychological, natural, normal? I'm a bit nervous of admitting my puzzlement and exposing myself to what may be a hostile, defensive reception but sooner or later I'll have to ask some questions.'

I was still smarting from a recent incident at the hospice when I had been attending a lecture. It was supposed to be about 'Spiritual Counselling' but it was all at a terribly dreary level and I was feeling a bit despondent. There was one woman there, all buck teeth and turquoise eye-shadow who announced herself as 'a Chris-ti-an' (she pronounced the word in three crisp self-satisfied syllables). She didn't have a question; she just wanted to tell us that she worked for some voluntary organization which gives cups of tea to 'drug addicts, homma-seck-suals, and other unfortunates', as she put it, and that because she loved Jesus she could love them too.

I'm sure she tried her best but I was repelled by her sanctimonious hypocrisy. She was one of those who later agreed with another woman, when the subject of nursing AIDS patients came up, that they had 'brought it on themselves'. One should feel sorry for the poor haemophiliacs . . . hard to be sympathetic to homma-seck-suals . . . I don't think I could bring myself . . .

It wasn't the occasion for a blazing argument but my heart was heavy at such a display of fear, ignorance and confused thinking. Certainly the lifestyles of some gay men have contributed to the spread of AIDS. All our lifestyles contribute to the diseases we get. Would you refuse to nurse a lung-cancer patient who had smoked all his life? A high-stressed businessman with a heart attack? A racing driver with a broken neck? The question is not one of how we can apportion blame but of how we can begin to see that good health is to do with taking responsibility for our own well-being. Reclaiming our own power, as Christopher Spence says; refusing to be a victim, having a reverence for our own bodies and a sense of our own worth.

I was annoyed with Turquoise Eye-Shadow, but I was also angry about my own confusion and inability to take her on in an articulate knowledgeable way.

All the more appropriate, then, that our next Lighthouse training session should be to do with the topics of oppression – particularly gay oppression and its relationship to AIDS.

One of the strongly held views of Lighthouse teaching is that we are all, in one way or another, both victims and perpetrators of oppression, and that our first task is to unravel the webs of misinformation we perpetuate.

We looked at the content of some of the misinformation about gay men which is rife: they are child molesters; they must have had dominating mothers; they must have been sexually abused as children; they are limp-wristed and fickle; they bitch and mince; they are weak, unstable and incapable of fidelity; they are amoral, promiscuous, pathetic, perverted, damned. 'At the very least, I hope my son won't turn out to be one.'

If you are a gay man, these prejudicies will result in deep-seated feelings of self-hatred, contempt and guilt: I must be wicked, sick, unnatural; I must be the only one; I might grow out of it; I'd better keep it secret; I can't be a real man, so I'd better act out butch or camp so that at least other gays will accept me . . . Isolated and rejected, you become defined by your homosexuality, dependent on the 'gay scene' for companionship – a ghetto which serves to reinforce your self-image and internal conditioning. Many of the clubs sell drugs, alcohol, porno gear. They are often dark and highly charged with anxiety and fantasy. People are encouraged to act out still further, even to the point of suicide. At the very least, the sadness and strain of living out these lies make them very vulnerable to emotional and physical illness. 'In the face of a virus which attacks the very immune system itself – the ultimate in self-destruction,' says Christopher Spence, '. . . we are profoundly vulnerable to the worst ravages of a disease which seems to confirm our worst picture of ourselves.'

Giorgio, a handsome young Italian, stood up to tell his story. I wept when he spoke about his obsessive search for the man of his dreams. As a teenager he had drifted into the macho leather scene – chains, boots, peaked cap, the whole uniform – and although simultaneously frightened and excited by the risks he took in countless bleak assignations, he always felt lonely and disappointed afterwards.

He had seriously considered suicide, but luckily found a sympathetic priest to talk to; his life-long isolation was coming to an end. The realization came to him one day in the course of a conversation that the man he was looking for – big, strong, broken-nosed, smelling of pipe tobacco – was the image of his father, a professional soldier. Giorgio's father, incapable of showing affection to his only son, had always kept his distance. 'I admired him so much,' said Giorgio. 'All I ever wanted was to be like him.'

Geoff had been standing very close to Giorgio, holding his hand as he spoke. He hugged him now as he began to cry. 'What would you have wanted from your dad?' he asked. 'Closeness,' answered Giorgio. 'What would you like to tell him?' asked Geoff. 'I love you, dad,' said Giorgio, and he sobbed in Geoff's arms for a full minute while I marvelled at his courage in being able to reveal something so intimate to such a large group of people.

We all adjourned to our support groups feeling very moved and very close. Neil spoke about his painful domestic situation: his lover, Frank, is in the final stages of AIDS dementia – difficult, demanding, bitter, jealous, horrible. Neil is finding it very hard to cope. Although he knows Frank can't help it, he sometimes just wants to walk out. But he doesn't. I thought about the astonishing loyalty and devotion being shown by so many gay men who are bearing the burden of nursing a friend or lover through to the end. We all cried with him and hugged each other.

I felt ashamed to realize that although I would never have thought of myself as an oppressor, I had subtly bought into the prevailing systems of social control and organization; creating false images and scapegoats, trying to ensure that someone else was lower down in the pecking order. As a woman I should know better; women have suffered in the same way. Lighthouse is playing a crucial part in dismantling these destructive stereotypes and reconnecting us all, whatever our sexual orientation, to a sense of our own individual worth, beauty, tenderness, expressiveness, humanity and feelings.

As the course went on it struck me with increasing force that the AIDS crisis has highlighted a general malaise in our society. It is an expression of a more widespread problem. Who *does* lead an 'immunosupportive' lifestyle? Never mind AIDS; an awful lot of the less drastic diseases are a direct result of 'immunosuppressive' behaviour. AIDS is forcing everyone to take notice; it is pointing the way to a more loving and honest, less alienated and fearful existence. And procrastination is no longer an option. The changes will come about when we adopt the attitude that everyone has the 'right to live'; the right to be happy and accepted and respected. People's stories of unloving mothers, violent fathers, sexually abusing uncles, unfaithful lovers, fairweather friends, add up to a lifetime of calamitous relationships and self-fulfilling, self-perpetuating expectations. The challenge is to break the pattern.

'Once we become human and stop wearing our different labels – "gay", "straight", "old", "young", "Catholic", "Jewish" – the things that separate and divide us from one another,' said Geoff our tutor, 'we can get down to business. The main purpose of Lighthouse is to contradict isolation and to guide people safely home.'

Staff at St Stephen's hospital believe that many AIDS patients die of isolation before the virus kills them.

5

> The tragedy of life is what dies inside a man while he
> lives   ALBERT SCHWEITZER

One day, some months after the course had finished, I received
a telephone call from Ted, a member of my support group.
The AIDS referral we had been working with, a fellow named
William Evans, had just rung him in a panic. He was feeling
very ill and frightened and alone and had no one to collect his
medicine from the chemist. Ted (who lived five minutes away
from him) was unable to go, which was why he had rung me.
Wandsworth is an hour's drive from my home and I really
would have preferred not to schlep all the way over there to
run an errand a minicab could have run, but I'd never done
anything for William – all the weight of his care and befriend-
ing had been taken on by Julian and Ted. So really as a
penance I agreed to go.

I picked up the prescription and went round to the tiny
fetid little flat where William lived just behind the prison. The
door was on the latch. Billy, as he liked to be called, was
squatting on his haunches in the corner of the room. Ema-
ciated and pale, hair falling out from chemotherapy, he looked
like a newly hatched vulture chick. He was surrounded by
little boxes of pills and tablets which he was sorting and
shuffling obsessively, dirty cups, half-empty bottles of sour
milk, and ashtrays overflowing with smouldering cigarette
butts. The place was a tip.

I sat down, not knowing where to begin. We faced each
other and made small talk. He apologized for the fact that I'd
come such a long way and that the place was such a mess. 'I
hear you're the one with the healing hands,' he said. 'I could

do with some of that instead of these.' He held up a handful of pills. His voice was slow and drugged and his eyes were glazed, as if he was trying hard to stay awake.

He looked like an inmate from a lunatic asylum in one of those nineteenth-century engravings; only instead of iron chains restraining him in the corner of a cage in Bedlam, he was bound by medical drugs. He told me he had been on Valium for seventeen years. He was now thirty. Once upon a time a doctor prescribed a strong tranquillizer to a mixed-up, difficult thirteen-year-old just beginning his adolescence and then threw away the key. We still persist in the fiction that silencing the symptoms will cancel the cause, that anaesthetizing the pain will alleviate the problem. Crazy? Awkward? Depressed? A misfit? Take these pills and you'll forget why.

Billy's flat was squalid, but it could be argued that he was being well looked after by our society. A social worker and a home help called in. When he got really ill he went into hospital. His Social Security money arrived. His housing was arranged. But at the heart of it some fundamental things were missing: time, love, physical contact.

I'd heard he was very unpredictable and could be extremely abusive and angry. But today he looked so lost and anxious that my heart went out to him. His main AIDS-related problem was a type of cancer called non-Hodgkin's lymphoma. He suffered pain all over his body for which he was prescribed strong painkillers, DF118s. These gave him constipation, he said, for which he took more pills which in turn made him nauseous, for which he took more pills. It was hardly surprising that he felt so rotten. He ate practically nothing, living on Complan and cigarettes. 'Why not try some prunes instead of more pills for the constipation?' I suggested helplessly. 'Oh yeah,' he said, eyes flickering briefly with interest, 'I quite like them.' But I don't think he could actually summon the energy to do anything for himself, so dependent had he become on 'them' giving him something.

Ted and Julian had obviously mentioned my interest in alternative medicine. He asked me about the kind of healing work I did and several times said he wished he didn't have to take so many pills. He asked a lot of questions. Was 'laying on of hands' sexual, he wanted to know, because touching of any kind meant sexual to him. No, it wasn't. Had he perhaps never thought that touching could also be an expression of love and care such as a mother gives to a little child? He snorted. 'Love was a dirty word in our house,' he said, 'let alone sex.'

He also wanted to know, half-apprehensively, half-salaciously, testing me out, if I was interested in the occult. Not particularly, I answered, briskly crushing that line of speculation in the bud. I said I thought it was a mistake to get bogged down in hocus-pocus. Healing, as I saw it, was actually a very simple process, a gift with no strings attached of loving energy channelled into someone in need, enabling them to recharge their own failing self-healing mechanisms.

I suggested that since he seemed so interested, he might like to experience for himself what it felt like, particularly as it could be a very good way for him to help himself with anxiety and pain. Where would he feel most comfortable? On his bed. He lay down with his eyes closed, breathing rapidly, shallowly like a hunted rabbit, body as tense as a piano wire. I held his ankles and feet and slowly talked him through a breathing and visualization routine. I worked round his body, holding all his joints in turn, finally placing my hands gently over his heart and his solar plexus.

Gradually he began to relax and breathe more easily. I took him on a magic-carpet ride to a place where a golden waterfall pours through the universe and we drifted through it in slow motion, basking and bathing in the particles of light. He really entered into the spirit of the thing and said he could feel the golden light flowing through his body. Tears slipped from his eyes and wet his pillow. Would he promise me, I asked, that before he took his next Valium he would try to recreate this scenario with the power of his mind? Just to see if it made a difference. Don't be a hero, I said. If you need it take it, but maybe you'll find you won't.

He asked me if I would come again and I promised to come every Monday when I finished at the hospice which was quite near where he lived. He put his arm around me and kissed my cheek. 'I feel great,' he said. 'That was marvellous.'

Every time I saw him over the next few weeks it was with a pang of recognition. I could see in his eyes, in his thin frame, so many of the young men I know, sons of my friends, my own sons, my nephews . . . Billy told me his life story. 'Hopeless family situation,' he said with a sardonic laugh. 'My father was a pompous, rigid Victorian. Liked me to call him Sir and thank him after he beat me.'

He ran away when he was fifteen, lived rough for a while earning enough to keep himself through a little amateur prostitution, fell in with some very bad company and finally took up with a much older man who was a heroin user. He hinted at some unspeakable experiences in the world of child pornography. 'I've brought it on myself,' he said. 'There's not a lot I haven't seen in this town and it's left me with a pretty low opinion of human beings. I can remember about two years ago saying to God, "I've seen enough, I don't want to live any more. Take me home."' Two weeks later he had been diagnosed with cancer.

Once he had wanted to be a social worker and help people, he said. Now he didn't have much regard for them. Didn't have much regard for anything. He told me about a recurring childhood dream he had had of being picked up by a giant, lifted high into the air and then dropped. Every time he was lifted higher, but he was always caught just before hitting the ground. 'One day I'll just smash to pieces,' he said smiling. 'It'll be a relief, actually; I can't bear the suspense.' A terrible psychic numbing seemed to have taken place in him – a defence against the unendurable pain and stress of his life. To live and to feel were too dangerous. The link between AIDS and lack of self-esteem seems to beg notice.

I talked to Billy about reclaiming his own powers, using his bright mind to harness his energy, making himself whole again. I could see he was attracted to the idea and excited by it, but also terrified by the implications of freedom and health. 'Too late,' he said. 'Far too late.' But I was spurred on by the knowledge that it was possible.

'Hope is a passion for the possible,' said Kierkegaard. 'A conviction that options exist. Faith is the courage, the *audacity* to act on the premise that all things are possible.' He is quoted in David Augsburger's fine book *When Enough is Enough*.

There is no magical release, no instant solution, no final satisfaction. Love is to be shared. Grace is to be received. You are loved as you are. What you are is enough. Just accept the acceptance. I didn't say any of this to Billy, but it was what I wanted him to hear.

The last time I went to see him he wasn't there, although this was a carefully prearranged visit. I left a note on his door, and he rang back later. His voice was heavily drugged. 'Oh sorry, thought it was tomorrow.' Was it a genuine mistake? Was he deliberately testing me? Or sabotaging himself? I couldn't help feeling a frisson of annoyance. One of the good things about belonging to a support group is that you can always call someone to blow off steam. Nobody has to try to be a saint in the face of frustrations and I had a good old grumble about wasting my time.

But the next thing I heard was that Billy was dead. Ted rang to tell me he'd died all alone in the flat. Oh heck.

The saddest and most damaged person I have ever met. Billy embodied all the anonymity, lovelessness and alienation that characterize our society. It was never tranquillizers he needed. His death made me angry at the way we short-circuit the child's natural gift for dealing with feelings. In our culture addictions are the accepted props for coping with stress and pain. As Christopher Spence said when he came to speak to our group, 'Powerful business empires have a vested interest in keeping the population hooked on these mind-numbing addictions.'

The result is that we no longer hear the voice inside us; the voice that urges us to be unafraid of life and death, that informs our finest thinking and prompts our boldest decisions, that sings our best songs, that celebrates our dreams.

'AIDS simply sharpens our choices,' said Christopher. 'Like nothing else in our lives before, it confronts us with the choice either to make our lives an expression of how we have been hurt and "disempowered" in the past or to make them a consistent eloquent expression of the decision to live well no matter what changes this will require us to make.'

The Greek philosopher Democritus wrote that 'To live badly is to spend a long time dying.' Billy spent a long time dying, but three of his Lighthouse friends went to his funeral and I believe he knew that someone cared about him at the end.

In contrast to poor Billy's living death, the story of Henry Tennant is that of a man seizing the moment. Everyone in this book has had their name changed and their identity disguised with the exception of Henry, who does not wish to be anonymous. He feels very strongly that standing up and bearing witness is part of his own personal challenge to make sense of the fact of AIDS in his life, and that by hiding he would only participate in the spiral of fear, shame and negativity which makes it more difficult to educate public opinion.

Henry is a 28-year-old man with AIDS. He is also a beautiful, gentle, exceptionally articulate and intelligent person. He is, as he says himself, already famous for having AIDS as his parents are close friends of the Royal Family. The tabloid press went mad when they found out, chasing him around town like a pack of hounds baying after a badger. Because he had grown up with a lot of press interest in his family it didn't bother him too much, but many of his friends felt shattered by this intrusion into their private lives.

I first met Henry when we chanced to enrol for the same Lighthouse training course and found ourselves placed in the same support group. We quickly got to know a lot about each other.

He was antibody positive then, the full-blown AIDS didn't develop until about six months later. He became very ill with bronchial pneumonia, spent a couple of periods in hospital and now lives with a frustratingly depleted store of energy. This is the hardest thing for him to bear, especially as he feels he has a great deal to accomplish and limited time in which to do it.

I had come to love and admire him very much and the thought that he might die seemed unbearable. No matter how well you think you are prepared for the possibility of loss, the reality is always different from the theory.

He wanted to contribute his thoughts on living with AIDS, so we recorded a long conversation.

'My reaction when I first knew that I had the virus was terrible despair,' he said, 'because my aspirations at that time were largely based on self-gratification. When I was first diagnosed with HIV I was in no way prepared for it. I was conducting my life on a very superficial level – one of self-indulgence – because I wished to avoid the experience of pain or unpleasantness.

'The helplessness I felt at being told I carried the virus was very heard to bear. My mind was a turmoil – No point in planning a future if I might not have one; no relationships; no sex; I'm all alone; no one will love me ever again; I feel ill; I'm sure "IT" is starting; everything's hopeless.

'I made myself much iller than I was. I'm the sort of person who's always been able to make myself suffer.

'At that time, a friend of mine who is a Nicheren Shoshu Buddhist told me that if I wanted to feel vitality in my life again I needed to discover a sense of mission or purpose. Worrying about my health, feeling fearful and isolated, was not the way to do that. In order to be happy again I would have to change my goals so that my life could *embrace* the HIV infection.

'The Nicheren Shoshu way is to chant. At first I was not impressed, I couldn't summon up any enthusiasm, I was overwhelmed by inertia and lethargy, but after wallowing for a while in self-pity I knew I had to make a choice and I was prepared to do anything to change my state of being – my state of mind.

'The thing about chanting is that it is a tool – a process of facing up to the realities of your life. It's a very powerful technique for revealing one's true character to oneself. It made me confront all my weaknesses: my inability to take action, my lethargy, my psychosomatic tendencies.

'A spiritual practice works because it makes you take responsibility for your life in a way that is terribly difficult to achieve on a purely intellectual level. What I chant is "Nam-Myho-Renge-Kyo", which expresses respect for the universal law of cause and effect which governs our lives. At each moment in life we are given a choice either to create maximum value for ourselves and our environment or to settle for something less. The choice we make depends on how angry we are or how fearful, how selfish we're feeling or how open and loving.

'As I chant I become more and more mindful of how the law of cause and effect works and how we are constantly making our own reality. It's a process of learning to be that open and loving person who will create maximum value.

'Once you recognize that you've only got x number of days to get your life how you want it, you really can't afford to waste a minute. The tragic thing is, there are lots of people with AIDS who have succumbed to a life of moaning and despair and feebleness. Because of their illness they feel they are living in hell. A healthy person naturally fluctuates between this state and a higher state of loving and learning, but AIDS or drug addiction, for example, mean that your life lingers in a state of suffering as opposed to a state which allows you to give.

'As a person who has AIDS – feeling ill a lot of the time, easily upset, easily swayed by negative values in life – I'm continually fighting my way out of a state of hell. It's possible to transcend those hellish states if you have the will and the discipline. After all you have to have a practice to maintain

109

healthy teeth. If you never brush them they will eventually fall out. It's the same with the way we behave and conduct our lives. If I didn't have some kind of practice to remind me every day that I've got to *be* this person that I want to be, I would quickly lose confidence in my ability to achieve it.

'It's been very difficult, but as time has gone by I've realized that I *can* change aspects of myself. It's a supreme alteration of attitude and perception – accepting death as my counsellor, living my life as though this were my last day. It's brought awareness into my life and I would like to think it's affected the people around me because they can see the difference it's made in my life.

'I hope and pray that people on a wider scale will adopt some form of spiritual discipline so that they can not only prevent their personal suffering but ultimately save the world, which won't be worth living in a hundred years from now if we don't do something about it. Today we live in an age of deep darkness and illusion where human beings are contributing to the destruction of their environment. Life is in imbalance. People are out of rhythm with the laws of cause and effect. If it continues, this planet will no longer be capable of supporting evolutionary life. This is happening as we speak.

'The crisis is so severe and there's so much at stake, we need desperate measures to wake us up. Mankind will either assume his rightful role as the loving guardian and protector of this environment or he will die out. The magnitude of the AIDS crisis is perfectly in tune with the times. It is perhaps the only thing we will listen to. It's a great inspiration for me to be able to shake people to do something positive, to be a pioneer. I hope I can play a useful role before I succumb, that I can help tip the balance in favour of the future.'

I thought of Robert Frost's poem, 'Stopping by Woods on a Snowy Evening':

> But I have promises to keep
> And miles to go before I sleep.

'As I become iller, AIDS becomes my life. I long to take a holiday from it – from waking up every morning feeling so lousy. But you have to accept the reality of your life and *then* create maximum value out of what you've got. I'm so much helped by my Buddhism because it gives me a strong and vibrant focal point which is *not* AIDS. A counterbalance which is dynamic, forward-looking, expansive, problem-solving. At the very time that your body is physically declining beyond repair, the most essential part of you is growing tremendously.

'I want to die in a state of true happiness. I want to die fully conscious and chanting. I want to be in control of my death and have people with me who know what kind of spiritual atmosphere I would like around me.

'It's a pity that society's current taboo about death, particularly untimely death, is denying us all an invaluable source of learning and personal development. We need death to savour life. Do what you can in the time that you have. You can't expect to be "normal" again once you're diagnosed with AIDS, but accept the fact that you can be changed by it.'

Shortly after we recorded Henry's thoughts, he took an amazing turn for the better, felt his energy returning, went away on holiday, got a job. He had dared to look death in the face, and now it retreated for a while, bearing witness to the powerful effect of finding meaning and value in your life. In seeing healing not necessarily as a cure, but as a way of becoming whole, Henry is bringing all his mental and spiritual resources into harmony with his body and actually strengthening his immune system against the odds. Once you fully own something you can choose whether you want to keep it or throw it away. You can't help what's been done to you, but you can choose whether or not you want to be a victim. It seems clear to me that what Jesus meant by 'turning the other cheek' was not a matter of passive complicity and resignation, but of active choice. The choice not to be a victim but actively to exercise forgiveness and responsibility.

Alan was an old friend from my journalism days – a wry, humorous Scotsman. I was sitting by his bedside in the AIDS

111

ward at St Stephen's Hospital in London giving his back a gentle rub; he had just suffered a rather miserable bout of PCP (pneumocystis pneumonia, the type most commonly associated with AIDS). He'd been longing for a bacon and lettuce sandwich so I'd brought him one, but he felt too awful to eat it. 'Some mornings I wake up and think to myself, "I could do without the challenge of AIDS today,"' he said ruefully. 'Sorry, I just don't think I can manage it.'

'It's these little things that are my only real regret,' he went on. 'Because on a wider scale, it doesn't matter any more if I get well again or not. I have become responsible for my own state of well-being. I am alive *now* in a way I never was before. Oblivion was what I used to seek – a tranquillizer for grief, alcohol for unemployment, a sleeping pill for a broken heart – and like a clown I acted the part that people expected me to play. I wanted to die. The rough, impersonal sex was a metaphor for suicide.'

Alan had been on one of the earlier Lighthouse workshops called 'Life, Death and the Challenge of AIDS' led by Christopher Spence. It was the turning point for him. 'Through learning to love myself for the first time ever,' he said, 'I can be just who I am each day. The journey is the greatest teacher, but I couldn't have done it alone. I think precious few of us, whether dying or trying to heal ourselves, ever manage to deal honestly with our pain without someone supporting us through it. People need each other.'

You have to do it for yourself but you don't have to do it alone.

Because the idea of AIDS is still so highly charged with horror and shame, the relatives of those who have died of it have a particularly difficult time. Parents may have heard all at once not only that their son is gay, which they never knew, but also that he is dying of a ghastly disease. The surviving lovers and partners of either sex may let themselves become very isolated – cut off from any source of human companionship or support.

112

Feeling that there is nobody they can tell, nobody to share the pain and confusion with, their own grieving process gets driven underground. They confront not only an aching sense of loss but also the very real terror that they might themselves be infected with the virus.

I got to know Ellen at a Lighthouse weekend workshop held on Raven's Ait, a pleasant small island in the middle of the Thames. There was plenty of time for talking and sharing as we sat outside on the steps of the boathouse watching a family of goslings learning to swim. In that sunny, peaceful place, far removed from the fear and prejudice of the world outside, the words flowed easily and companionably like the waters of the river flowing past us. I heard the story of a beautiful love affair and the way it continues to enrich her life.

Ellen and David met eight years ago. They were best friends, sharing the vicissitudes of an actor's life in a touring theatre company. 'To be honest,' Ellen said, 'the real love I felt for him only came in the last year after he was diagnosed. If he hadn't got AIDS it would have been a different relationship – we'd have carried on being best friends.

'David was my guide and mentor. He encouraged me and helped me, he made me bolder because he believed in me. He was the most amazing good fun and managed to make a joke out of all the appalling things about being on tour – the ghastly digs, unloading lorries full of equipment in the rain, first nights with nobody in the audience. We had those exhilarating, exciting conversations which go on all night and you don't bother to go to bed. I'd never known anything of that depth before.

'Our sexual relationship was very intermittent and not hugely important. Another way of being friendly. Just a game really. So much of the so-called promiscuity in the theatre is just because you need a cuddle sometimes when you're far from home. I'd always known he was gay – it didn't worry me in the least. I knew how special I was in his life. Even when he was in Pitlochry and I was in Penzance we were always in close touch.

113

As far back as 1984 Ellen and David had been aware of AIDS, and they became involved with the Terrence Higgins trust after a dancer they knew got ill. 'I guess at the back of my mind I'd always thought that doing fund-raising and such – being part of combating it – would give us an immunity. A protective magic to keep it at bay.

'Then one day David went to the clinic about a minor infection he'd had and the nurse said, "By the way, we did the HIV test on you and it was positive." Just like that. No counselling. Nothing.

'We felt we couldn't tell anyone because there was such a lot of anti-gay, anti-AIDS feeling in the community. We spent the weekend holding each other and crying a lot. Only afterwards did it dawn on us that I was also at risk. "I don't believe this," I said to myself. "It can't be happening." It was like watching myself in some terrible disaster movie. "I can turn over the channel if I don't like this," I thought. But I couldn't.'

Ellen had the test done and it was negative, but she was sent a recall a month later saying there had been a muddle over that batch of tests and not to rely on the results. She decided not to have it done again, mainly because both she and David believed that he might never have got so ill if he hadn't known he had HIV.

'Within a few weeks of the diagnosis he was beginning to get minor symptoms. His landlord found out and slung him out of the flat, his parents were awful, and as he didn't want his friends to know, we were thrown together even more. Because there was such a definite sense of shame I got used to keeping it quiet. I'd just landed a rather nice part in a TV drama series and I knew I'd lose it if anyone found out.

'About that time someone gave me a copy of Christopher Spence's article 'AIDS: an issue for everyone'. I approached Lighthouse, offered my services and started attending a course, but I was heavily into denial at that time and I didn't release any of my feelings. I never told anyone there that David was HIV.

'At Eastertime, only five months after the diagnosis, a

114

hospital visit confirmed he had advanced Kaposi's sarcoma internally and it was beginning to break out on his face. That meant full-blown AIDS. The treatment was appalling: chemotherapy – including AZT – radiotherapy; all awful because they made him feel so bad. I was going crazy commuting back and forth from the TV studios in Birmingham. I loved the job and it was my big break, but instead of being the springboard to everything, it had become a terrible burden. I just wanted to be with David. There was no choice really. Knowing that it would probably be the end of my career, I quit.

'AIDS focused the relationship so completely; it turned it into something it hadn't been before. It heightened and highlighted the precious qualities. I realized that you can lose the things you take for granted. He gave me a ring and we even talked about getting married, but there was suddenly no more time.

'At this point David was given the option to go on to a new drug – a daily injection with horrible side effects. If he took it maybe it would extend his life a bit more, but it would make him into a permanently ill person, almost institutionalized, having to attend the hospital every day. Even though it felt selfish, I wanted him to decide not to have it, because as it was he had periods of feeling fine and this stuff would turn him into an invalid. I wanted whatever time we had left to be quality time. The doctors wanted more guinea pigs and put a lot of pressure on him, but he chose not to have it. At the end of June he got pneumonia – PCP – and the doctors said it was his fault for disregarding their advice.

'He was scared and he knew he was dying, but at least one of the few fringe benefits of knowing you're going to die is to be able to organize things the way you want them – to be completely in charge. We talked quite a lot about the funeral he wanted and chose the hymns he liked – much to the astonishment of the vicar, who was rather embarrassed by all this advance planning.

'More than anything else David wanted to travel to the Lake District one last time, to say goodbye, so against

115

everybody's advice we booked a self-catering cottage for July and one night in a posh hotel. He felt very weak and couldn't walk more than a hundred yards from the car, but it was a magical, extraordinary, romantic time. It's what I look back on with the most pleasure. I was nervous about going because I thought, "Oh God, I'm just going to cry all the time." And we did cry, but not too much. There was a lot of laughter and a closeness completely unmatched. It was beautiful and I thank God that we had that.

'On the last day he collapsed. His lungs were filling up, he couldn't breathe, couldn't stand. I called the local GP, who completely freaked. He couldn't cope at all, wouldn't even call an ambulance, and insisted that I take David to Manchester General Hospital in the car. David's parents were informed, and they arrived in the middle of the night screaming abuse at me for killing him by refusing medication. You wouldn't believe the awful things they said. They insisted that the medical staff proceed with active treatment and ignored David completely.

'For the two of us, while this bizarre soap opera was going on over our heads, it was a time of tremendous closeness and silence. He was drifting in and out of consciousness but he would occasionally grin at me and had the energy to squeeze my hand. He wasn't speaking, but I heard him say without words, "They don't have to keep trying." He was down to six stone and it hurt him every time he took a breath.

'For his sake, I just wished he'd die, and eventually I said to him, "Well, what are you waiting for? You can go now." I was able to give him that permission and it worked. At five a.m. I was sitting by his side and he just stopped breathing.'

The sun went down beyond the bend in the river and a heron flew past. The goslings scuffled among the reeds on the bank. Ellen paused for a minute or two and hugged her knees, rocking gently as the rekindled memories filled her voice with tears. She wiped her eyes with an old scrunched-up tissue and we silently put an arm around each other.

'I'll say what I think happened next because it's all I know,' she continued. 'Our telephathic communication at that stage of his dying seemed to be stronger than ever. That's how it had always been with us anyway, throughout the eight years we'd been together. Distance was no barrier. I'd ask what I should do and I'd hear him telling me. Now, as the elements were leaving his body one by one, we had this conversation for twenty-five minutes although I know he was already dead. He asked me what I'd do and I told him I'd go to the Lighthouse. I wanted him to know that my antibody status didn't matter, that if I was positive I wouldn't blame him.

'After about a week I plucked up courage to ring Lighthouse and the isolation began to end. They were shattered that I'd never told them and had been bearing the whole thing on my own. A couple of times a week I received wonderful counselling that made me start crying properly for the first time. I told a whole group and nobody ran away. I started to heal.'

Unemployed and absolutely broke, Ellen started crusading for Lighthouse because she wanted to see a change in public opinion. Now she works in the new hospice building as a full time co-ordinator and campaigner and is making a huge contribution to the lives of many people with AIDS.

'Something of David inspires what I do now. I can connect with that last twenty-five minutes we had of unspoken communication. I don't ask him questions but I do hear the answers. When I'm thinking "Do I dare?" I hear "What's keeping you?" I couldn't be doing what I'm doing now without him. There's a sense in which we complete something of the life of the one we loved as we live on with the strength of what was shared. It's a dedication – a memorial.'

When I visited America in 1980, shortly after the massive volcanic eruption of Mt St Helens in Washington State, I had the opportunity to fly over the smoking ruins in a friend's two-seater plane. The devastation at close range was shocking to see. Thousands of acres of forest trees had been flattened – they were lying like spilled matches on a carpet. It looked as

117

if the end of the world had come. But the following spring an extraordinary photograph in the *National Geographic* showed new green shoots pushing their way up through the tons of grey ash. It reminded me of the Easter hymn:

> Love lives again that with the dead has been
> Love is come again like wheat that springeth green.

On that Raven's Ait weekend, one of the most powerful and unforgettable experiences was the informal Sunday morning celebration of the Eucharist led by Tim McKenna. Tim is a gentle and loving man, a Roman Catholic priest who worked for many years with an overseas mission in the Far East. Not long ago he discovered he had AIDS and decided there was no option but to tell his superiors. Instead of being allowed to use his pain and suffering as he would like to be able to, continuing to serve as an even better priest, he has been thrown out of the church. Quite apart from anxieties about his health, his sorrow is immense and the frustration of being cut off from his vocation very hard for him to bear. We took a ferry to the other side of the river and went for a long walk together. I valued his humour and his eloquence, and when he told me he was going to hold a Mass on Sunday morning I knew I would want to be there.

It was held in the library and not many people came: three gay men with AIDS, three extraordinary nuns and a Jew (me). We put our chairs in a little circle and held hands. The feeling of love and compassion and the real spirit of Christ were very much present. Tim's theme was the idea that weakness and vulnerability often turn out to be our greatest strengths. If Jesus were alive today I feel sure He would have approved. He would surely be living amongst AIDS patients, bringing his love and courage into the place where there is most suffering.

Geese flew past the window, rabbits hopped about on the tow path, the little votive candle burned brightly and Tim passed around the sacrament. I didn't eat the body and drink the blood of Christ because Catholicism is not my belief, but

I loved the beauty of the service, its celebration of love, and its affirmation that anywhere can be a place of worship if two or three are gathered together in the name of truth and light.

6

For what is it to die but to stand naked in the wind and melt into the sun? And what is it to cease breathing but to free the breath from the restless tides, that it may expand and seek God unencumbered.   KHALIL GIBRAN

'There's more to death than dying,' said Mr Bob Dedman with a saucy wink. The aptly named freelance embalmer had come to give a little talk to a group of nurses at the hospice. It sounded like the cue for a song, and indeed his black leather jacket, gold chain and white slip-on shoes reminded us that he had once worked as a professional entertainer. Embalming was more rewarding, he said, not to mention more lucrative, and he kicked off with a droll story about a woman who had kept her dead husband in bed for seven months with hot-water bottles and electric blankets until he dried out into a block of wood.

An embalmer's skills would give a more reliable result, he told us, as well as guaranteeing a more natural-looking finished product which could then, if one so wished, 'be preserved in an airtight casket, in a mausoleum.'

Apart from an embalmer's purely practical role (the body of anyone dying in a foreign country, for example, has by law to be embalmed before it can be repatriated), his services are most often called upon to make the deceased 'as presentable, peaceable and pain-free looking as possible'. It takes about half an hour to embalm an ordinary body. The arterial system is injected with pink-coloured formaldehyde which 'gives a natural, living look', wrinkles are removed, the features are arranged into a little smile and all evidence of death is erased.

Part of Bob Dedman's training was a course in make-up at Leichner's. 'I'm happy when I hear someone say, "Oh doesn't he look younger!" or "She looks like she's only sleeping!"'

A more complicated commission might involve rebuilding features, 'complete heads if necessary', using plaster of Paris and a wire cage to supplement what's left of the bone structure and covering the lot with plastic skin ... Bob Dedman's manner was slickly matter-of-fact and he'd evolved a grotesque Monty Python jokeyness. This was probably essential to his sanity, but it was surreal in the extreme to listen to.

'Doesn't all this make the denial phase harder to get over?' asked one young nurse, but her question was brushed aside.

I found the whole thing very macabre. The price we pay for our materialism and technological cleverness is a profound alienation from the fundamental fact of death. I was reminded of Woody Allen's remark on his fortieth birthday: 'I shall gain immortality, not through my work but by not dying!' which sums up the Western approach to death. It need not happen, and if it does there must have been some mistake.

This is why it was so refreshing to meet Sophie.

Shortly before I was due to take my summer holiday she was brought into the hospice. Because she had consistently refused all medical intervention – surgery, chemotherapy, radiotherapy – for her lung cancer, she had somehow been forgotten, and was found lying in abject squalor with her confused and elderly husband, both of them completely unable to manage. She had been the more practical one of the two, but now that she was too weak to shop or cook, they were literally starving.

When I saw her I thanked goodness for the existence of hospices. The nurses got her care and treatment just right and she was given whatever her heart desired (real filter coffee and rice pudding) to make her last days dignified and comfortable. Her unusual personality was recognized and acknowledged.

Her cancer was now very advanced and she was close to death, a skeleton weighing only four stone. Her hair was matted, her eyes were gummed up, whiskers had sprouted all around her face and a gigantic tumour was growing on her neck, but she was still alert, witty and articulate. Her skin was too tender to be touched anywhere so massage was not appropriate, but I sat with her for hours on end talking or being silent – whatever she wanted – and I found her a great inspiration. I learned a lot from her remarkable acceptance of death, an attitude I'd always felt and hoped was possible.

Sophie was a very sharp, intelligent, fiercely individual woman. She'd lived her life with reckless gusto and was approaching her death in the same way. She was a sculptor, a genuine Bohemian, who had lived in Paris in the thirties with artists and writers and still thought of France as her spiritual home. The child of Jewish immigrant parents, she married an ultra-Englishman 'in an attempt to disguise myself as a pukka English woman. But it didn't really work. I can play the part faultlessly for about three hours and then they sus me out! I never feel I really belong here.

'I've always been a gambler and a risk-taker. Do you know that line from Shakespeare? "Our doubts are traitors and make us lose the good we oft might win by fearing to attempt!"' She lit another Benson and Hedges. 'I was perfectly aware of the risks of cigarette-smoking too, but I loved to smoke. I gambled and lost. Gamblers shouldn't whinge when they lose. I couldn't bear to be rescued. I don't want them cutting me up to save me. This is the natural outcome of my life and I'm genuinely interested in the process of dying. I only hope it won't be boring after all this. I'm excited by what lies ahead. My bags are packed and I'm ready to go.'

All her talk about dying rather upset the other patients. 'As usual, I don't really fit in,' she said. 'Banquo's ghost at the banquet. An embarrassment!' She laughed. I admired her for her bravado, her defiance and her provocative remarks. Her body had become a terrible encumbrance to her, she said, and she was longing to be released from it. 'And yet something makes me hang on in spite of myself. I don't know what I'm waiting for. I always was the last person to leave a party!'

She loved to sleep now, she said – everything else required

too much energy – and described a special dreaming state she kept slipping into, unlike any she'd ever known, wherein she was already half out of her body. It was a state of great lightness and peace, and she looked forward to it. 'It's like a rehearsal and not at all frightening. I can smell hay and roses and I just hope the real thing will feel like this.

'I'd always hoped to have my ashes scattered at a sacred site like Stonehenge, but now they've ruined most of them with car parks and wire fences. My next choice would have been France, but I don't much like the idea of some French douanier with a Gauloise hanging from his lip sifting through my urn at the border for cocaine!'

Sophie was philosophical about the decay of her body but also talked about the irony of how vain she used to be, how sexy; how she loved beautiful clothes, how gorgeous her legs were. Those legs were now propped, swollen and suppurating, on a raised cushion ('like a stick insect in moonboots' was how one of the other volunteers described Sophie). 'None of it matters.' She smiled a wonderful smile. 'I know I'm not this body.' I thought of Rembrandt's portraits of old people: inside the crumbling flesh the light is shining.

'I have a young friend, a disciple of the Indian guru Bhagwan Shree Rajneesh, who comes and talks to me about non-attachment,' said Sophie. 'He still has a long way to go because he doesn't laugh enough, but he's on the right track and speaks the truth. "If you have lived just a bodily life and you have never known anything beyond the body," he told me, "death will be an anguish because the body has to be left behind. If you have lived a little higher than the body, if you have known love and loved music and poetry, if you have looked at the flowers and the stars and something of the non-physical has entered your life, death will not be so bad, although even then you are having to leave behind things you are attached to. But if you have touched something of the transcendental in yourself, if you have entered into the nothingness at the centre of your being and everything simply *is* as it *is* – just pure awareness, consciousness – then death is going to be a great celebration, a revelation. Death is no longer death but a meeting with God."

'Apparently the face of one dying Sufi mystic, at the very last moment, became almost supernaturally radiant. His disciples had never seen anything like it. "What is happening?" they asked. "God is welcoming me," he replied. "I am going into his embrace. Goodbye." I like that idea. A date, a love affair with God.'

She knew I was going to France the next day for a country wedding and she was envious. 'If I could have one wish it would be to feel entirely well for one whole day and to enjoy a last glorious meal sitting outside under a grapevine at a country restaurant in France.' She sighed, but not sadly. 'Eat some lovely food for me,' she said. 'I wish I'd met you sooner. Next time perhaps we'll have a bit longer together. Goodbye and God bless.' It was the last time I saw her alive.

I toasted her with a glass of champagne in the beautiful French summer countryside and she was there in the warm smell of hay and roses. I thought about her all day, wondering if she could feel the connection as strongly as I did. The next morning I rang the hospice to speak to her and was told she had died the evening before so I'll never know, but in my heart I shared that day with her.

Sophie had talked with such assurance about going on, about the end of this life being the start of a great new adventure. What gave her that certainty? Her dreams she saw as a preparation, a preview. My mother too had vivid dreams shortly before she died, mostly of landscapes where she'd never been. There was always a light of great intensity and a feeling of welcome, a feeling of coming home. She dreamt once, she told me, of a stage set like a split-level room. She was waiting in the wings and all the other actors, my father among them, were on the upper level sitting round a table where an empty place was laid for her. They were beckoning for her to join them but she couldn't remember where to come in.

Having been close to many people now at the moment of

death, I have a much stronger belief in the continuation of consciousness than I ever had before.

Ultimately, of course, we only get to know the full story when we die, but there are now many recorded testimonies from people who have had near-death experiences, who have been pronounced clinically dead by all the usual medical criteria but subsequently come back to life again.

Just as I was thinking that it would be a good plan to investigate this further, I heard that there was to be a four-day international conference on 'Life After Death' in London, so I went along. A young friend has coined the term 'Crusties' – Cranky Upwardly Spiritual Triers – to describe the type of New Age loony he thinks I am in danger of becoming; but the fact that loads of ordinary people have had remarkable spiritual experiences can't be dismissed quite so easily!

I guess that all of us would secretly like to hear someone say, 'I know there is an afterlife and here is the proof.' I don't think it's unreasonable to piece together little snippets of other people's visionary sagas to make a colourful and cheerful patchwork.

Dr Raymond Moody has interviewed over a thousand people, mostly cases of cardiac arrest, who have had near-death experiences. Although the subjects came from all walks of life, their experiences fall into a very definite pattern. Typically, after hearing a nurse say, 'We've lost him', or 'He's gone', or 'Oh my God he's dead,' the person has a radical change of perspective. He becomes a spectator, watching his own body and all the resuscitation procedures from some external vantage point.

'It's as though they rise above the physical body,' said Moody. 'They witness in great detail the heroic attempts being made to revive them.' The senses are somewhat altered but they 'see' and 'hear' quite clearly everything that's going on – what order people come into the room, for example; even

what is happening in another room. One woman eaves-
dropped on her relatives *outside in the corridor* and heard them
whispering, 'Looks like old Vi's kicked the bucket at last.'
They were highly embarrassed when she subsequently made
her re-entry cackling with glee and telling them to be a bit
more careful what they said next time.

What convinced Elisabeth Kübler-Ross that this couldn't
all be explained away in neurological terms was her own
experience of being at the deathbed of a woman who had been
blind since childhood. She was able to describe with complete
accuracy the colours of the clothes people were wearing
around her bed after she 'died'. When she left her physical
body she could see again with her inner eyes. Her 'astral' or
'etheric' body was restored to its former undamaged condition.
She was whole again.

I was extremely interested by one man's tale of his own
drowning. There was a point, he said, when he had left his
body but could still look down on it thrashing about. 'The
reflex physiological surivival instincts were still working over-
time; I was like a chicken running around with its head cut
off, but I was gone,' he said. 'There was no pain, no panic,
though it must have looked terrible to anyone watching. I was
looking on with detachment and compassion and it certainly
looked terrible to me.' He was pulled out of the water dead –
no breathing, no heartbeat – and given mouth-to-mouth
resuscitation for over an hour by two people. The first, a
Chinese boy, left the scene before the storyteller regained
consciousness, yet he could describe him in some detail
without ever having seen him.

I found that story very comforting: it implies that what may
seem to an outside observer to be a painful or distressing
death might not be so to the person experiencing it.

People reported that they had difficulty believing they were
really dead and that the lifeless body used to be theirs. 'A
cutting of ribbons', one person described it as. 'You are no
longer the spouse of your spouse, the child of your parents,
the parent of your child – you are you in a very pure form.'

126

Released from the pressures that shape and the ties that bind, the essence is free like a genie let out of a bottle.

I have come to believe that a person in a coma knows exactly what's going on, that the conscious self continues to think and perceive, and it also seems to me possible that this stage persists for some time after clinical death.

I recalled again my own certainty that my father's presence was still in the room in the hours following his death. That same night, although exhausted by the terrible events of the day, I had been unable to sleep. Consumed with grief and shock I lay restlessly tossing about with my mind racing, longing to turn the clock back, regretting all the things I hadn't done for him, wishing I'd been able to say goodbye, furious with myself that I couldn't remember even one of the wise little aphorisms he was always coming out with. Then suddenly, clear as a bell, I heard his voice inside my head saying, 'You can't stop the birds of sorrow from flying about your head, but you don't have to let them make nests in your hair! Be happy, my precious Lali.' There was nothing super-natural about it. It was a real, ordinary voice, and the words were so vivid and so typical of him, it made me smile. A great feeling of warmth and calm came over me and I fell immediately asleep.

One man, a mechanical engineer aged thirty-five, told how he had tried to commit suicide with pills, whisky and gas after an unhappy divorce. He described in great detail his death and the clear understanding that came to him, when he left his body and went through the tunnel many people who have 'died' describe towards a great light, of how he was not going to escape anything by pulling out. Lessons still had to be learned and pain suffered. He saw a new way forward: 'It can take forever to change your ego by one millimetre on a psychiatrist's couch – a glimpse of eternity can change it in a flash,' and when he realized he still had a choice, he returned to his body, somewhat reluctantly and fearfully but in the knowledge that it must be so. The experience had utterly changed his perception of the meaning of life, he said, and made him a much more loving and less self-pitying person.

'Before that, I felt the world was such a black, bleak place that there was only one choice left; all the others had been cancelled and there was no way but out. Now, having experienced it for myself and seen the effect it had on others, I know it is not a route I would ever allow myself to choose again. I was seeking oblivion because I was afraid to accept life. But oblivion is not what you get. You can't run away from yourself. I had a glimpse of what hell must be – the unleashing of the demons of the mind, all the unresolved pain, all the meanness, all the unloving actions. Dying was not going to solve anything. Now that I have looked into my death I have seen that I must dare to be open to life.'

Moody commented that although people who attempt suicide often try again, those who have a near-death experience never do.

I was struck by the extraordinary parallels between these accounts and the Tibetan concept of the Bardo of Dharamata, the 'dark night of the soul' – that stage in the process of dying when the 'demons of the mind' are unleashed. The demons that surround you need to be recognized for what they are: the subjective instincts and forces of the human personality. Recognized and let go.

'When your body or ego dies, what you experience is the true nature of mind,' said Sogyal Rinpoche, the Tibetan teacher who spoke at the conference. 'When the blockages die they explode in visions. If you realize this early, before you die, it's quite useful. Don't be frightened; it's just a release of energy. When you look into the meaning of death you find the meaning of life. It is a mirror. It is essential to the vitality – to the life force – of spirituality. When you transcend death, you find life. That is the meaning of the resurrection. Death is meeting ourselves.'

Sogyal peppered his wisdom with a disarming humour. 'I'm on to a good thing,' he said, laughing and beaming benevolently. 'Death is becoming fashionable. Everybody's doing it!

Death and healing go hand in hand; if I don't succeed in one I'll succeed in the other. A one hundred per cent success rate. I can't lose!'

In the West, he reminded us, thinking is said to be a sign of intelligence but it can make us dumb – 'so clever we miss the point'. And to illustrate the extreme opposite he has invented a character he calls Monsieur Maintenant who is so intent on 'nowness' that he never gets round to thinking at all. 'The middle way is what we aim for,' he said. 'Not too much or too little – just enough.

'Life is a collection of changes and impermanence and the brain is a mechanism for protection – holding all the impermanence together. The biggest mistake we make is in trying to make the impermanent permanent. Our difficulties all come from not really believing in impermanence. It always comes as a shock, especially in someone close to us.

'Modern man sees death as the enemy of life, and the fears build up. We can dispel them because fear is all in the mind. Death is not depressing; it is inspiring. Out of death comes life. Out of understanding comes real birth. Thinking of death cleans your life and makes you more ready. Procrastination feeds on the illusion of permanence and speed gives an illusion of progress – we are always running, running. Again, look for the middle way. Because we do not know why or when or how we are going to die we pretend it can't happen or will come later – at the end of your life span. But who knows what your life span is? Better to be ready.

'Although this life is important it's only a small part of the whole of eternity. While we have this precious human form we have a chance to work out all our life's patterns. Look into death – keep it in the centre of your heart and it will make your life much fuller. Just *dying* is not it: We will all do that successfully! The main thing is how will you be with yourself when you die?

'Death lives! It's happening all the time. Life is ticking away like a bomb. Most people have a tremendous endurance for suffering but very little capacity for happiness. They don't recognize it or use it and when it's all over they say wistfully, "Those must have been the good old days." Like the man trying to boil water in a wooden bowl, they end up with nothing.'

So what to make of it all? Moody had always been sceptical himself, he said, knowing how easy and tempting it is to sensationalize and embroider this kind of testimony. He asked himself all the questions I would want to ask: Are these experiences elaborate fantasies? Intellectual constructs? Self-delusions? Defence mechanisms to assure us of a wonderful world to come and save us from the reality of annihilation? His first thought was that there had to be some rational explanation for them – hallucinogenic drugs, temporal lobe epilepsy, mental disturbance, cerebral anoxia (lack of oxygen to the brain) or endorphins (the endogenous morphine compounds – natural painkillers produced in the body which can cause altered states of consciousness). But each one of these explanations failed to account for the way people so accurately describe their resuscitation procedures.

From the moment they spark back into life again and reunite with their bodies, people who have 'died' report profound changes; transformation, in fact. Life is more appealing, more meaningful, and at the same time there is no longer any fear of death. There is a feeling that life is really worth living in this world but also that there is something more to come.

As the conference went on, more and more parallels between the near-death experience and *p'howa* emerged. One woman spoke of feeling that she had condensed into a tiny speck of consciousness travelling upwards, '. . . then "I" was free. I had left my body. I had projected in space somewhere above the bed on which my inert body still lay. And I knew this was what the world calls the state of death.'

What seems to be going on outside yourself may turn out to be a reflection of what's going on inside – echo-soundings from the layers of symbolic and collective experience we harbour. I remembered Chagdud Rinpoche saying that it was only our cock-eyed concepts that created boundaries between

130

inner and outer in the first place; that the traveller, the path and the destination were all aspects of oneself. The *p'howa* practice is a conscious attempt to have a near-death experience.

Dr Moody said that as a psychiatrist his main job was to help people leave behind their unhappiness and neuroses. He was fascinated by the fact that a near-death experience completely removes a patient's neurotic anxieties and short-circuits the long psychoanalytic process. 'People are moved along to a higher level, and often made to confront quite painful aspects of their lives.

'It's very difficult to explain away NDE features by any known phenomenon,' he said. 'And although I don't believe our findings have been adequately proven yet, my own inner self, my own heart is convinced that my informants have had a glimpse of the beyond. The only difficulty is that often nobody will believe them. They fear ridicule and are reticent about discussing it. There is a tendency within the medical profession to dismiss NDEs as psychosis, but I say they have to be taken seriously. NDEs have nothing to do with mental illness; they represent a profound encounter with the deepest level of self.'

'I became aware that I simply *was*,' said one woman. 'I didn't have to do anything. When I realized I was going to lose everything I had ever known, I had no option but to surrender to my inner being.' A medically trained pharmacist, she had 'died' in the terrible car crash which killed her two sons aged nine and eleven. After the impact, she experienced moving upwards 'at tremendous speed, through what looked like the tornado in *The Wizard of Oz*. As a life-long agnostic, all the time I was saying to myself, "This can't be happening, I don't believe this," while I looked down on the blazing wreck of the Peugeot. I saw, in minute detail, people pulling my body out and the boys trapped in the back seat, and *at the same time* the three of us were already leaving together. That's when I knew that the real me would not die with my body. I was still there, we were still there.

131

'I encountered, on the other side of the whirlwind, a wise presence – not a person so much as a shimmering radiance, a core of wisdom – and was told – no, "told" is not right because there were no words involved; "absorbed the understanding" is a better way of putting it – that Angus and Tom had completed their life's work and were free but that I had not.' She had argued and raged but the longer she resisted it the more difficult it became. 'I finally accepted and acknowledged that the "wise presence" was probably an aspect of my own inner being, my higher self, and that as soon as I stopped standing in my own light the problems would disappear.

'Without knowing the purpose, the boys died and were allowed to go on. And I died, but only symbolically – to my former way of life – and had to return. Does any of this make sense? When I revived, my life took on a different meaning, a commitment. I'm still a practical, level-headed person, but whereas before I was dogmatic and argumentative, now I let the universe take charge of my life. You don't have to be in charge,' she said. 'You just have to be.'

She has turned her house in Canada into a therapeutic community for adolescents with drug problems, travels around working as a healer and therapist, and feels she has been enabled to do something of greater worth in the world. 'I miss my family but I actually know they are all right and that they did not suffer in the fire.'

Somebody asked her if she could still contact her two sons. 'No, not in the sense you probably mean,' she answered, 'but I sometimes see them in dreams or as sort of tree sprites. I've thought about this a lot. In my mind they remain forever little boys because that's the only way I can picture them – it was the only guise I knew them in – but that was over ten years ago. I often have a sense of them like a warmth around my heart. My guess is that the personality as such probably doesn't survive. Since it is created in this life, we maybe grow through it and out of it – each of us a one-off, all leading to the development of a greater transpersonal self. I think my

132

little boys have found their way back to the infinite unity from which we originated. What surives is the energy and the love.'

In trying to understand how to live more comfortably and less fearfully with notions of death we probably learn a lot more about life. All the people who spoke of their experiences stressed the philosophical and ethical changes that had taken place in their lives, the lessons they had learned, and their clear realization that status, wealth and material things are not the most important goals in life. Only the love you show others will endure or be remembered. The 'encounter with the deepest level of self' enables you to see clearly the actions of a lifetime and to understand the consequences and effects they have had on others. Seeing this in the presence of a non-judgemental 'companion' (the Being of Light, your own Christ consciousness) has the effect of making you want to reach that understanding again and to live your life by it.

One woman who bled to 'death' giving birth to her only child was miraculously resuscitated. 'It doesn't really matter what's going on in your body because you're not in it any more,' she said. 'I was summoned back to look after my newborn baby and for his sake I'm glad he didn't have to be an orphan, but even my brief glimpse of what happens after death made it very difficult to re-enter this world willingly. I came back because I had to, not because I wanted to. I will never again be afraid of dying.'

Margot Grey, who has written a book stemming from her own life-changing near-death experience, ended one of the conference days by leading us in a powerful meditation on our own death: 'Curl up in the arms of Mother Earth and leave your body in her arms.' I was instantly transported back to the memory of a lullaby my mother used to sing me. I loved it and begged her to sing it but it always made me cry (it still does). It always triggered the memory of a huge and lonely vastness in its melancholy minor mode, and even when I was a very little child it fired me with intimations of infinity. Time and space expanded in all directions around me . . . 'Do you want the stars to play with?' I did, but I was afraid. 'Or the

133

moon to run away with?' Would I get back by morning? 'They'll come if you don't cry.' But she wouldn't be with me and the sky was cold. 'So lula lula lula lula bye bye, in your mammy's arms be creeping.' I was safe for the time being wrapped in the warm smell of Je Reviens and Dans la Nuit which she used to mix together. 'And soon you'll be asleeping, lula lula lula lula lula bye.' I cried because I knew she would die one day and there was nothing I could do to prevent it. Life was like that and we had to learn to be alone.

Looking back now, I know it was then that my conscious internal history began to blossom and fuse with my ancient wisdom. I was already connected to the void. It seemed to stretch back to the time before I was born and forward into time to come, across the borderline between the known and the forgotten. I was part vulnerable, part indestructible, part human, part spark of divinity, with one foot in this world, one in eternity. I saw the universe as a great and mysterious living creature and all of us people as cells of one vast being. Now here in the middle of Regent's Park I curled up in the arms of Mother Earth, and when the meditation was over I found my face was wet with tears.

What is the difference between hallucination and revelation? I guess the answer is that what you receive is pretty much the same. The ear with which it is heard – heard spiritually, heard metaphorically – and the way in which it is interpreted, are what make the difference.

The view that human beings are merely electro-chemical computers does not adequately account for the relatively common 'mystical experience' – the feeling that one is somehow on the verge of the mystery, in the presence of something greater than oneself:

As I came down the hill into the valley across the golden meadows and along the flower-scented hedges a great wave of emotion and happiness stirred and rose up within me. I know not why I was so happy, nor what I was expecting, but I was in a delirium of joy; it was one of the

134

supreme few moments of existence, a deep delicious draught from the strong sweet cup of life. It came unsought, unbidden, at the meadow stile; it was one of the flowers of happiness scattered for us and found unexpectedly by the wayside of life. It came silently, suddenly, and it went as it came, but it left a long lingering glow and glory behind as it faded slowly like a gorgeous sunset, and I shall ever remember the place and the time in which such great happiness fell upon me.

Francis Kilvert's Diary, 24 May 1875

Are we really to believe that everything takes place in the brain? Can the world really be explained entirely by physics and chemistry?

In the late nineteenth century, science tended towards a definition of reality as that which could be measured by instruments. It was based on a materialist world view, and it seems that the concept of the spirit, the concept of quality, were not properly taken into account. But partly due to the work of Einstein and others on relativity, first physics, then more of science shifted ground. Fritjov Capra in *The Tao of Physics* explores this mystical thread which is pulling science back to a wider reality. In the sub-atomic world where there are no solid particles, merely probabilities, matter and energy are apparently interchangeable. This led him, and other contemporary physicists, to a state of awe, for they were finding proof that when we speak of 'the light within' we are nearer the truth than we imagine – we really are made of light, condensed into matter.

The scope of science is gradually widening, and neurologists will one day be able to integrate what people experience in coming close to death with what they know of brain function, but as yet the nature of consciousness is largely ignored because we don't have a method of measuring it. Maybe if we take the pressure off the mind for a bit instead of constantly trying to fit everything into a known frame of reference, we can accept our feelings. These are perfectly valid and don't have to be backed up with logic. Science has no way of explaining some of the things we take for granted – subjective experiences such as hunches, intuition, precognition. Like being in love, they can't be proved, but that doesn't alter the facts.

One of the areas of exploration most bedevilled with charlatanism, nonsense and sometimes pure vaudeville slapstick is that of mediumship – trying to get in touch with the dead after they've 'passed over': the world of mysterious thumping, wobbly tables and Madam Zaza straining her ears into the ether. Although quite happy with the symbolic concept of communication, I've always felt uneasy about the *literal* interpretation of this phenomenon. Communications from the spirit world are invariably banal. Big public sessions with famous mediums are more like radio phone-ins:

'Is there anybody in the audience whose name begins with M?' 'I've got a Ronald or Donald here who says thanks a lot for the lovely flowers and tell Mum to keep warm.' 'Missing you all.' 'Weather's nice.' 'Love to aunty.'

I accept the importance of comfort and reassurance, but I am also aware of the extreme vulnerability of bereaved people and suspect that they have provided rich pickings for unscrupulous exploitation from time immemorial. When you want to believe, you'll swallow anything.

I mentioned these misgivings to my friend Heather, a very wise and articulate woman of eighty-six, who dismissed my fears as irrelevant. In the face of grief, any comfort which the individual finds helps him and which harms no one else must be a good thing, she said, however strange it may seem – having a good cry, attending a seance, becoming a Roman Catholic or taking up pottery. 'For consolation comes in unexpected ways and no one need be ashamed of the humbler ones, from a cup of tea to the trite sayings that tell us that ours is, after all, not a lonely but a common human experience.'

On the other hand, thoughts in one mind *can* telepathically appear in another. The strength of one's connection to a beloved person doesn't die when they do; the relationship continues in a different form. A sensitive clairvoyant could possibly be of great help in picking up what is going on and expanding one's sensory awareness, enabling one to finish grief work and move on.

A young man who had had an unhappy relationship with his father told of how he had refused to be at his father's death bed because of his unresolved anger over his parents' divorce, his father's defection and subsequent remarriage. After his father died, the remorse and sorrow of all the unsaid words between them weighed heavily on his heart. He now has regular sessions with a medium during which he 'speaks' to his father, who has forgiven him and told him he is proud of him. A great deal of good healing has come about in the confrontation of guilt and pain. But how to explain what's going on?

'Proof', said Heather, 'is only for solving problems – questions which have answers. The ultimate questions are of another sort. They have no final answers, only way-stations which sooner or later must be passed. Ours is the intermediate realm between proofs that cannot tell us whether or not the garden is enchanted, and inspiration which shows us face to face that it is.'

When an experience is inexplicable in ordinary terms, it may be best to explore its symbolic dimension and accept that there are meditative and visionary states which are part of time, and yet lifted out of time – sacred spaces in which dynamic, healing change can take place. Anyone who, even for an instant, has felt the living presence of someone who has died and felt the compulsion of their sweetness, power, eloquence or greatness of heart, has penetrated that sacred space; and so has anyone who has responded to a string quartet, a line of poetry or a painting.

A man who had lost his only daughter asked Brenda Marshall from the College of Psychic Studies if it was wrong to try to contact people who had died – 'Should we maybe just let them go?' 'Immoderate grief holds them back and holds us back from living,' she replied, 'but wanting to know can't hurt anyone. Love makes the contact. If the most real part of a person is not that which shows on the outside, she won't change just because she's shed her body. At the heart of all religions is the truth about continuing life. But this is where the trouble starts. We must beware the trap of words because the truth is never static and it's notoriously difficult to pin down.

'Thought is an extremely powerful creator and a great deal of mediumship is not communication from the other world but a tuning in to our own truths, our own wisdom. Spirit people represent our own depth, a sea of consciousness we can dip into. The integrity of the searcher is paramount, and the real need is to find a reference point inside oneself.'

Coleridge expressed a similar idea in his notebooks: '. . . I seem rather to be seeking, as it were *making*, a symbolical language for something within me that already and forever exists, than observing anything new.'

Life after death? What does 'after' mean when there is no time or space? Perhaps 'beyond' would be a better word – life beyond life. An elderly friend of mine wrote to me recently following the death of her beloved husband after more than sixty years of marriage: 'With each new death – and at eighty-five I now experience many – I try to find out why I cannot "accept" it as we're told to. Physically of course yes – I already feel I've lived too long to adjust to all the stages and quick changes. But the sudden, final and unexplained disappearance of the personality along with the worn-out body seems at variance with the spiritual development.

'We know the mainstream of life is love, and we know we don't love even our dearest well enough . . . yet the better we love the more we suffer with each death. The first "lesson" of love, even in babyhood, is communication. Yet it is cut off by death – because we don't know what comes after it . . .'

The pain of grief, the mystery of death, the frustration of

138

questions that cannot be answered in terms of this life's experience, the search for explanations and clues to assuage our fear and anxiety are what make the testimonies of people who have approached death such compulsive listening and so valuable. They are like the accounts of early navigators trying to map the hidden shoals and reefs in uncharted waters. They may not be a hundred per cent accurate but they are better than nothing.

'The answer is probably within us and among us but we are not constituted to see it. We only understand what is within the orbit of our senses. We know there are non-sensible things but we can't get a grip on them. They are at the limit of our perception.' Rabbi Lionel Blue was speaking from a Jewish perspective. 'In Judaism there isn't much about the Afterlife. The accent is more on how you live this life. We cannot love well in this life unless we also continuously invest ourselves in eternity. We live in many realities – one of these is the reality of eternity, but it makes demands. A certain giving-up is required. You have to do something for someone else. Now is as good a time as any to start. You get back what you put in.

'We invest too much in objects. We focus our hopes on winning in the world of two-dimensional reality, but there are worlds of more dimensions than we can imagine. Somewhere inside us we know that death is not the end. This life is very enjoyable but it's not home. It is not quite complete. On a Jewish cemetery is inscribed "The House of Life". In the silence is eternity. Without that other dimension we can never find meaning or happiness in this world. We have to learn to be happy in a finite situation while reaching towards the infinite.

'Heaven is not a place; it is a state. You need to break through your own ego to that other dimension. The reality one serves and that which one is joining are all part of the same continuum.'

I loved his gentle practical widsom. His conception of simultaneous realities struck a chord with Chagdud's teaching

139

that the division between what was in us and what was outside is illusory.

The threat that if you don't have a religious belief of one sort or another you are doomed to a less glorious sequel has always seemed unfair to me: either buy a ticket or it's a one-way journey to nothingness for you. This reduces religion to an insurance policy – like believing in Father Christmas. If you don't, you might not get any presents. Blackmail. The writer Peter de Vries stated the atheist's position in an acceptably poetic way. He was not seeking 'meaning' or 'eternal life', he wrote, just a delight in the passing moment which is not too far removed from the Buddhist perception of awareness and non-attachment:

I believe that man must learn to live without those consolations called religious, which his own intelligence must by now have told him belong to the childhood of the race. Philosophy can really give us nothing to believe either: it is too rich in answers, each one cancelling out the rest. The quest for meaning is foredoomed. Human life 'means' nothing. But that is not to say it is not worth living. What does a Debussy arabesque 'mean'. Or a rainbow or a rose? A man delights in all these things knowing himself to be no more – a wisp of music and a haze of dreams dissolving against the sun. Man has only his two feet to stand on and his own human Trinity to see him through: Reason, Courage, Grace. And the first plus the second equals the third.

Avery Weisman, a psychiatrist, pursues the theme:

To find significance in death we must find significance in our own transience. In a very short time we shall all be nothing – a mossy gravestone somewhere, a few ashes in the sea. The rhythms of nature and the uncertainty of being alive bear witness to how we can mourn, forget and be immersed in man's anonymous continuity, like waves breaking against the rocks, challenging time and nothingness.

140

Arguing about belief systems or lack of them seems a foolish waste of time. Whatever explanation you come up with is as good as any other so long as you don't try to impose it on anyone else. You'll find out soon enough.

My own feeling echoes Erikson's concept of 'basic trust' – a childlike confidence in the integrity of life. My vision is of a benign universe, which allows me to face the certainty of death and its sequel. I feel that a flexible philosophy of life is a much better bet in the long run than a rigid ideology or creed. In the first place it is always open to revision and in the second the objective 'truth' of it isn't particularly important. What is important is how useful and comforting it is to me.

Working with dying people has made me confront thoughts about my own death. When I was younger I was much more flippant. I hardly ever thought about dying and when I did it was a case of everything ends and that's that. Anyone who believed in an afterlife was kidding themselves. The only possible immortality was the continuation of your genes in your children. And yet . . . all the doors I open seem to lead into bigger rooms, and I now feel certain that 'I' am more than this body I inhabit.

As the notion of total extinction, oblivion, nothingness has receded, so has my fear. Does belief create the fact? Do we create our own realities? Or is Elisabeth Kübler-Ross perhaps right when she says, 'Those who can hear will hear, and those who cannot will be pleasantly surprised when they make their transition.'

One hospice nurse read us this poem by a patient in her care:

> Do not stand at my grave and weep.
> I am not there, I do not sleep.
> I am a thousand winds that blow
> I am the diamond glints on snow
> I am the light on ripened grain
> I am the gentle autumn rain.
> When you awake in morning's hush

I am the swift uplifting rush
Of quiet birds in circled flight;
I am the stars that shine at night.
Do not stand at my grave and cry.
I am not there. I did not die.

7

I felt that if all the tears of the suburbs were shed, it would never stop raining.   CHRISTOPHER SPENCE

One cold March day a car skidded on an icy road and hit a child standing at a bus stop. He was rushed to the nearest hospital and the emergency team did everything they could to save him, but the injuries were too extensive and his life slipped through their fingers. A doctor came in, glanced at the little body, said not a word to anyone but wrote 'NEGATIVE PATIENT OUTCOME' across the file, leaving the nurses to deal with the hysterical parents and their own despair.

I heard this story from Celia, a nurse who was there that day, now a fellow participant on a workshop given at the Bristol Cancer Help Centre by Jean Sayre-Adams. 'It was the last straw,' said Celia. 'I had become increasingly depressed by the denial, the euphemisms and the professional alienation. Now I knew I didn't want to work like this ever again. I want to change myself; I want the cold, unloving medical and technological system to change from a business back to a healing art.'

She had come to hear of Jean Sayre-Adams' work, as I had, through the grapevine, and jumped at the chance to catch up with her on one of her rare visits from America. Jean is a nurse in the casualty ward of a big American hospital but now travels the world for part of the year teaching and counselling in the field of death and bereavement, drawing on her own horrifying personal experiences of grief and loss.

When her own baby died many years ago, she was not encouraged to talk or rage or cry; indeed, she was forcibly prevented from doing so. The dead baby was dragged from her arms, she was slapped across the face and told to get a hold of herself. 'So I did,' she said, 'but at great cost.' There was an embargo on the discharge of painful emotion. It was bad form; 'bearing up' was approved. She was given Valium to sedate her. 'Nobody wanted to hear my pain so I shut it away and there it stayed like a splinter of ice. The message I got was "If you persist in discharging, being difficult, being mad, you'll get taken away." Eventually it got so that even if someone offered me a Kleenex when I was crying I saw it as a signal that they wanted me to stop – and I would stop, and screw the lid on tighter. Everything about that time was bizarre and insane. It was as if the baby had never existed. I carried on nursing, but even though I was very dissatisfied with the way we in the medical profession handled death – appalled – I still couldn't hear the universe speaking to me until I was hit again.'

When Jean's seventeen-year-old daughter was killed in a car crash the conditioning of a lifetime prevailed. Her grief was locked up and inaccessible; she couldn't shed a tear. Knowing that it was crucial to her very survival to be able to grieve, she tried to help herself. She even worked with Elisabeth Kübler-Ross, but although a lot of good work was begun, still she could not let go. She was literally petrified – turned to stone. Her strait-jacket of self-control held her in its relentless grip until, at a friend's suggestion, she went on a retreat into the desert with Stephen Levine and Ram Dass . . .

'Learning how to keep your heart open in hell; that's the essence of Stephen's work,' said Jean. 'And there in that desert wilderness we undertook a very difficult practice: breathing and opening our hearts while watching a gruesome video which is shown in California to drunk drivers – a montage of people killed in road accidents. I saw my daughter with her head smashed open on the pavement and at last I exploded. An ocean of anguish engulfed me. Everything crashed around me. I thought I would die from the force of it. At some level of consciousness I was dimly aware that when the sea wall finally burst, someone in the room was breathing my pain with me – matching me breath for breath, holding, panting, gasping, sighing, staying softly with me in an embrace of breath, focusing entirely on me, on where I was. Not trying to change anything, say anything, offer anything – just being alongside. My healing had begun.'

It was Ram Dass who, with a quiet mind and an open heart, sat with Jean through her suffering. Her cataclysmic re-entry into the world of feelings changed the direction of her life and caused her to ask the fundamental questions that now form the basis of her healing work.

'How *do* we deal with suffering? I asked myself. Because there's no end to it. Even if we get past our own, we're into the collective. We live in a world of suffering. Every five seconds a child dies of starvation. One of the ways we cope is to push it away. Make a wall. Keep it outside. Or we label it the will of God or karma; we say it's "meant to be", so our hearts close down and we become impotent.

'Another way we cope is pity: "Poor thing! Thank God it didn't happen to me." Or, and this is often one of the hardest responses to unravel, we become "helpers" in order to get our own needs met. We get uncomfortable so we make ourselves busy, we want to change things, wish it could be different. But it's an endless task. You give and you give until you become angry and burn out and then you're no good to anyone. This happens to many people in the medical profession.

'Gandhi was right when he said, "Anything you do will be insignificant but it's very important that you do it." It's also very important to be aware of your motivation. As I see it you have no right to tell others how to live their lives or die their deaths. All you can do is to meet them at the place where they are. We need to meet that hell with a quiet mind and an open heart. People can die healed. People can live through loss and be whole and transformed.'

'When your fear touches someone's pain it becomes pity,' said Stephen Levine. 'When your love touches someone's pain it becomes compassion. No words are necessary. There's a saying in New England: "Don't ruin the silence unless you can improve on it!" Do not be afraid of the eloquence of silence – it is often a higher form of communication.'

At this point, a few people shared some of their own experiences of grief and bereavement which bore out this truth. An elderly clergyman spoke about his long journey back to living again after the death of his beloved wife. 'My healing began,' he said, 'the day when I met an old friend in the street. He said nothing but he embraced me, leaving some of his own tears upon my cheek.' A woman who had sat at the bedside of her little girl, who was dying of leukaemia, told of a neighbour who used to come in and sit with her every day for an hour or two, not feeling the need to make conversation, just keeping her company. 'Nothing would have made it any different or the sadness any less, but she was able to stay with me in my pain and I will never forget that.'

Here in Jean's workshop we tried a synchronized breathing exercise, working in pairs, trying to create an atmosphere of total accord with our partners. One of us lay down with our eyes closed and, breathing in our own rhythm, meditated on our innermost pain. The other one of us sat alongside with an open heart and matched every breath with our own, not asking any questions, not saying anything. 'Pain can't be measured,' said Jean. 'There's no worse or better – it's there, and when we sit in our suffering all we want is not advice or pity but for somone to hear us.'

It was quite extraordinary how this simple but powerful device created an instant psychic link. No words were necessary and the details of the individual sorrow didn't have to be spelt out; you could attune to the feeling. There was no effort involved, only stillness, and a telepathic intimacy flowed between us such as is normally only known by lovers or mothers and their babies. Once the trust and safety had been established, we stayed with each other silently all through dinner and actually fed each other. It was a very strange sensation but it was important, I felt, to experience the possibility that one might well need to be able to accept such a service with grace one day. Who knows the extent of helplessness we might have to face?

I remembered being moved by a documentary film about a women photographer who had made a series of searingly honest portraits of herself, staging events and scenarios from her past in an attempt to recreate and come to terms with the emotions they recalled: phototherapy, she called it. She portrayed herself as a baby; as a fat, middle-aged woman lying in the bath; as a greedy, compulsive eater; as a patient recovering from breast cancer ... and ended with a daring series of photographs, staged by herself and her man, showing each of them looking after the other in a state of complete dependency – having to be fed, dressed and have their bottoms wiped. It was a brave undertaking.

Jean's work is built on her conviction, which I share, that you can't be much use to someone who's dying or grieving until you've got some of your own stuff cleared out. The work on yourself never ends, of course. With every door you open there are ten more confronting you. 'As our consciousness expands we realize that what is within is without and what is without is within,' said Jean. 'All you have to take to a dying or grieving person is yourself and your open heart. If you come with fear, guilt, advice, self-righteousness, you will not be a safe place. If you come with stillness and compassion you will be a channel through which a healing energy can flow.'

I was reminded of a lecture I once attended, the theme of which was why human beings seem to have a perpetual need to create scapegoats and enemies. The speaker was Adam Curle, a political mediator and government peace negotiator. He told the story of how he once had to pay a visit to a big, fierce guerrilla leader with a reputation for violence and irrationality. He was quite physically frightened but mentally prepared himself before the meeting by meditating on their common humanity and managed to expel his own fear and revulsion. In order to break the entrenched patterns of mistrust and enmity it was necessary, he said, to have a strong belief in 'the common humanity that joins us all – atman, the

Hindu concept of the Godself, the compassionate wisdom, the innate goodness within everyone.' Atman is one of the most basic concepts in Hindu philosophy – the eternal core of the personality that survives even after death, the divinity that we all share. Adam Curle's emphasis was on listening as an active process. 'We need to remove the inner obstacles to peace,' he said, 'stifling our own need for self-justification, sinking beneath the surface to the level where we can reach the other person.'

I was very impressed by the quiet courage of his philosophy. I am well aware that to talk about unconditional love and an open heart is one thing at the bedside of a dying person; in a guerrilla hideout with a machine gun aimed at your head it takes a lot of conviction to believe that negativity can only survive on more negativity and that you will win because love is stronger than hate.

Adam Curle, faced with the 'enemy' and meditating on his common humanity, is doing the same sort of thing as a healer who has opened himself to the flow of unconditional love energy and can pass it like a current of electricity through a malfunctioning body or a congealed emotional state to stimulate the recipient's own self-healing powers. I know it's 'only in the mind' – an accusation often levelled at this kind of work by those who are uncomfortable with mysteries, along with 'purely psychological' and 'make-believe' – but it's none the less powerful for that. Make-believe can become make-happen.

Everybody, if they think about it for a minute, would accept that mental images can tune up the body's functions, prompting a physical response and altering the body's chemistry. The healer (or peace negotiator) is concerned with how the process can be made to work in reverse to undo tension, soothe pain, restore balance, heal disease.

We did a deep meditation on keeping the heart open in hell. We were to go deep inside ourselves and acknowledge whatever it was that caused us the most pain. 'What has been your wounding?' asked Jean. 'We don't share it for many different reasons – often because other people try to change it. Nobody lets go of anything until they are completely ready – until it has stopped serving its purpose. Try to get away from judgement, comparison, reproach, shame, guilt,' she said. 'What is, is. Just contact it and breathe into it.'

Breathing played a powerful part as Jean led us through the meditation. Every in-breath: life; every out-breath: death. We re-create ourselves constantly. 'At the still point . . . there the dance is,' she quoted. 'As you reach the furthest point of the out-breath you die and begin again; you are flowing and changing and constantly renewing. In: movement; out: stillness. In: light; out: dark. In: focus; out: diffuse.

Jean combines these breathing techniques with visualization, 'therapeutic touch' and practical tips. 'Find the little things that will give a dying person pleasure,' she says; 'plants, music, nice smells. Bring a baby to visit, or an animal. Change the lighting, perhaps, or move the bed nearer to the window, putting up a bird table where it can be seen.' All obvious, of course, but how often we forget the most obvious things.

The term 'therapeutic touch' was coined by Dr Dolores Krieger, professor of nursing at New York State University, with whom Jean studied. This is a modern version of the oldest healing known to man – one human being touching another with kindly intent. Therapeutic touch assumes that living creatures are open systems into and out of which streams of energy flow. These get depleted in illness and can be given a boost by contact with another person.

It has been found that patients in hospital who receive this attention on top of regular nursing care do significantly better than others which shouldn't surprise anyone any more than the latest startling research I read showing that tiny premature babies tend to do rather well when tucked skin to skin inside their mother's blouses instead of being wired up inside a temperature-controlled glass box. ('I could have told them that,' said my friend in the wool shop, the mother of nine children.) The healer, friend, mother, nurse are all calling on the same simple human capacity to harness the natural, harmonious energy of the cosmos and spark a healing response.

When one is working with dying people, the same principles apply, only the emphasis shifts subtly from healing as cure to healing as reintegration and reorientation at a deeper level, where the legacy of a lifetime of unfinished business has created blocks and disharmony.

To be enfolded in deep empathy and acceptance is a balm and a delight. We were all each other's healers, and although I've done this many times before, the experience of giving and receiving 'therapeutic touch' was freshly wonderful – miraculous, in fact, because it gave a feeling of utter certainty even to the most cynical amongst us that the power of human warmth is invincible and nature is even more astonishing than we dare to dream. Anybody can heal and have every degree of 'higher consciousness'. You don't need to do anything about it except appreciate what you already have and get rid of the things that block you from realizing your potential. Healing is not inexplicable; nor is a belief in it irrational. It is a natural law-abiding process. A profound empathy between healer and patient allows harmonizing energy to be channelled through the healer to the healed in a deliberate act of will.

'The only requirement if you want to help someone is that you like him,' said Elisabeth Kübler-Ross. 'You don't have to love everybody but you do have to like them. Trust your intuition and do what comes to you without judging or criticizing.' She also talked that day about her concept of the 'four quadrants' of which we are comprised: physical, emotional, intellectual and spiritual.

Dying patients obviously have physical needs that have to be taken care of. People should be pain-free, conscious and in a loving environment, in the company of children or music or whatever they want. They have emotional needs – the unfinished business of fears and phobias and doubts – that you can help them resolve. They have intellectual needs which require that you answer their questions honestly. (When, as a young doctor, Elisabeth Kübler-Ross first began doing research with dying patients she was asked by the hospital authorities to give an undertaking never to tell any patients they were dying. 'I never had to,' she said. 'They always told me!') But the fourth quadrant, the spiritual, you don't have to do anything about. 'It will emerge of its own accord,' she said, 'when everything else is in harmony.'

I was soon to learn the truth of this. Terry, a young friend dying of AIDS, had been very unhappy in hospital. Kaposi's sarcoma was all over his lungs as well as on the outside of his body. The hospital had put him on an intravenous drip but his veins were all collapsing from over-use. His medication was making him feel ghastly and he was retching himself inside out with terrible nausea, but he was surrounded by people who kept reassuring him that he was going to be fine. (This relentless pretence is sometimes referred to as the 'horse on the dining-room table' syndrome. Everybody knows it's there but they're all trying to pretend it isn't.) When I went to see him he had an enormous needle stuck between his ribs and a horrible yellow fluid was being drained out of his lungs. He was very confused, showing only occasional moments of clarity, and the further the illness progressed the more strangely he behaved.

By the next time I came to see him he'd had enough of wires and tubes. 'I've decided that death is not the enemy,' he whispered, exhausted. 'This terrible torture to try and save my life is far worse.' He had made up his mind that he didn't want any more painful or unpleasant invasive treatment, so the medical staff had taken all the drips and drains out of his body. He was on morphine now and waiting to be moved to a hospice. The hospital was not a peaceful place, with dinner trolleys banging, cleaners crashing about the ward, clicky-clack heels purposefully striding the corridors. It was the sort of place where dying was to be avoided at all costs.

Terry asked me to rub his back and drifted in and out of consciousness, restless, agitated, with his eyes half-open. His mind seemed busy, his lips were moving, and every once in a while he'd wake up with a start and look around him, trying to register who was there – making a supreme effort to focus his thoughts. When he did speak it was very hard to follow the thread; like the words that tumble out when you wake up suddenly from a dream, it sounded like nonsense. People tried to humour him but it was only frustrating him more.

The startling difference I saw in him the following week was entirely due to the beautiful atmosphere in the hospice to which he was finally sent. There, nourished by physical comfort, emotional sustenance, and enough honesty to satisfy his need for truth, his spiritual life finally came together. Brought up a rather reluctant Jew, he suddenly knew very clearly that what he'd wanted for a long time was to become a Christian; he had always lacked the courage to say so for fear of upsetting his parents. He wanted to talk to an understanding priest. 'I've always loved Jesus and I want him with me when I make the transition,' he said simply.

He found himself thinking a lot about his mother, who had been dead for ten years, and he kept dreaming of strange landscapes he'd never seen. 'I see my mother's face and know it will be all right,' he said. 'I see Jesus with his arms open wide and know that I can melt into his heart.' His whole frame of mind had changed from being agitated to being at peace with himself. He'd found what he wanted – the human face of compassion – and his mind was dissolving into the wisdom mind.

On one visit to the hospice, I saw a young nurse with a face like an angel come into Terry's room just before going off duty and kiss him good-night. It was a gesture of infinite tenderness and acceptance. He was barely conscious but he smiled and lifted one hand weakly in acknowledgement.

I think this definition of a healthy person makes a fitting epitaph for Terry, who died a couple of days later:

He has learned to use all his energy for forward motion and self-realization. Not self-centred, self-conscious, or selfish. Singularly free from the defence mechanisms that are often used to protect a person against false hazards and non-existent enemies. He has freedom from either fear of the future or remorse about the past and he has released his psychic energy to make the most of the present.

The morning Terry died, John Shine, one of the co-founders of Lighthouse, sent me a beautiful piece he had written for its monthly newsletter.

... We live in a society that pretends death doesn't happen. It's also true that in Britain 80% of people who die do so in acute hospital beds. As a nurse, I know that hospitals are not geared toward people dying ... Dying at home or in a centre of excellence are just two of the issues around which our organization is setting out to create a new model.

I would like to share one of our recent celebrations. His name was Graham. I first met Graham about two and a half years ago in one of our groups. He had been diagnosed with Kaposi's sarcoma. It was ironic that Graham, who was a very good-looking man and set a lot of store by his looks, should end up with such a disfiguring disease which caused more lesions on his face than there was normal skin.

Graham died last week and shortly before this he told us that these last two years have been the best years in his life. I remember once asking him the question: what was good about having AIDS? He said: 'I realize that this diagnosis of AIDS presents me with a choice either to be a hopeless victim and die of AIDS, or to make my life right now what it always ought to have been.'

One of Graham's greatest challenges was his isolation, and he was determined to conquer that before he died. And he did. Just two days before, he arranged his funeral in every detail. He then finally decided to let go and I took responsibility for his medical care in the last 24

153

hours of his life. He was able to die in the comfort of his own home, surround by the very people he always wanted to be there when he died.

We set the room up with candles and incense and played music that he liked very much – in particular 'Room with a View' – and what a view we had in that room! We had made up beds on the floor all around Graham's bed, so that his friends could lie or sit. By this time he was unconscious but very peaceful, and we were explaining everything to him as we went along. His friends enjoyed taking part in his nursing care, and his mother never left his side. She lay next to him on the bed all through the night. He died so peacefully that it was hardly noticeable. We just stayed with him; there was nothing more to do. The candles burned on, the music played and people cried. Graham's wishes were carried out in full.

After some time, his friends helped me to wash him and lay him out. We laid him in the centre of his double bed, with his two soft toys, one each side of his head, which were gifts that he cherished. People took turns to lie next to him, love him and say goodbye. It was music to my ears to hear his friends say that they would never be scared of their own deaths. We kept him at home until the afternoon, and just spent the time celebrating him on his way, singing songs and hymns, having some tea and toast. One young man with us had been Graham's Lighthouse volunteer and had become a very good friend to him. He had spent almost every day with him since June, and continued to care for him right up to the end by assisting in his laying-out. He said this experience had completely changed his life.

Helping Graham to die so well has been a pleasure and a privilege. It brings us all closer to our vision of how it could and should be for everyone. It's all very simple really.

The terrible story Christopher Spence told of a beloved friend of his who died in 1984 was very different. This man was in the last stages of the illness and wished to be allowed to die quickly, but he was admitted against his will to the isolation ward in an intensive care unit. Barrier nursing with masks and space suits reinforced his impression that nobody would want to go near him with a barge-pole. There were no home comforts, not even a picture on the wall, and no one was allowed to visit him. Medical people went on and on intervening, and he eventually died on a ventilator, lying on a trolley with disposable paper sheets.

'It was not good enough,' said Christopher. 'It was horrible. People need somewhere to die decently and decide for themselves the nature of their death and how to live the last of their lives.' He added that the reason he himself now lives the life he wants is because he has dared to look at these issues. 'The centrality of death and the way our lives are touched by it connects us to what we may be.'

In order to be able to help a person die well it is clearly much more important to know what sort of a person is dying than what sort of terminal illness he or she has. When I returned to the hospice after the summer break I was told by one nurse that 'two new breast cancers and a bladder' had recently been admitted. Fortunately this kind of labelling is not common in hospices, but it shouldn't happen at all. The people who were living in these failing bodies were, in fact, a thirty-eight-year-old mother of three children, a very old blind lady who had once been an opera singer, and a retired electrician whose wife had died three months previously. They all had their own, unique life stories, their own qualities, their own joys and sadnesses, and each would cope with the fact of death differently.

Most people are not so much afraid of death as they are of a *bad* death. But it seems to me that there are two closely related issues to be considered here. The first is getting clear that it isn't a question of 'if' or 'when' or 'of what' we're going to die but of how we're going to live today. The second is to reorganize things so that more people have the opportunity to grieve well and to die well like Graham and Terry. After his beloved friend died and Christopher was bereaved, he found that people couldn't listen to him for more than a minute before they became fidgety or started talking about deaths in their own lives. The subsequent workshops he held on death, dying and bereavement disclosed a tremendous need. People came in droves to cry and to tell their stories.

Loss is a built-in fact of life. We die and are reborn each moment. 'We suffer and go through the death process every time we lose something,' said Jean, 'but death brings rebirth and we have the ability to re-create ourselves constantly. Every moment you live is precious. Not until you can live each day as if it were your last can you accept death. When we truly understand this we attain liberation and power over death. It is essentially our own ignorance that keeps us in bondage.'

Every change involves loss. The harm comes from not discharging the pain of loss (and this is where our secular, buttoned-up society falls dismally short), which results in an awful lot of ill-health, morbid fantasies, mental breakdowns, even suicides. 'We don't talk about death and loss; we use euphemisms instead,' said Jean. 'Funerals are cursory and impersonal. We think that we are not meant to have much say in the procedure so we hand the ceremony over to professionals.

'It's in our interests to get rid of all this nonsense. And although I always feel it must be particularly irksome to people with HIV or AIDS to be told it is a blessing or a gift to humanity, it is quite possible that the whole AIDS crisis may forge this overdue, sane move towards making it possible again to die at home naturally with people who validate you.

'Take death inside of you – make death your lover,' she added provocatively. I thought again of those medieval illustrations of death; of a knowing-looking skeleton locked in an intense fandango with a maiden; of them whirling through life together, flirtatious, inseparable, intimate. Death was once a familiar and constant dancing companion, a part of life, not the ultimate 'negative patient outcome'.

One sensitive young policeman told us how, disillusioned with the dubious joys of maintaining law and order, he had quit the force and become a nursing auxiliary. His fearlessness and physical strength, made him an indispensable member of a hospice outreach team. Steve's pitch was Central London, and many of the people he cared for were homeless drifters, tramps, drunks, drug addicts – people dying in lonely doss-houses, hostels, squalid bed-sits or, more than once, cardboard boxes underneath the arches of Waterloo Bridge.

His job demanded a lot of fortitude. The dying people he was called out to could be aggressive and abusive. They were quite often dirty and smelly, lying in their own vomit, clothes soaked in urine. He had been doing this for two years, and as there was a negligible support structure for the carers in his team, he felt exhausted and depleted. He had come on the workshop in the hope of replenishing his own heart. What had motivated him in the first place was a desire to help and heal, but he had been told by his superiors that his job definition most certainly did not include counselling in any shape or form. That was to be left to 'qualified people'. Talking with patients, beyond day-to-day pleasantries, was discouraged 'because it invariably leads to your getting drawn into their messy lives', he was told. He was on no account to discuss the patients' illnesses with them; decisions about what or how much to tell were to be left entirely to the senior doctor in charge of the unit. Violation of this cardinal rule would lead to instant dismissal. So long as he understood that his role was little more than that of a meat porter, lifting, carrying and cleaning up, he would get along just fine. It was in his own interests to be quite clear that detached non-involvement was the only way to cope with the considerable demands of the job.

He was young and inexperienced so he did as he was told. But then he broke the rules. One day the outreach team, consisting of a social worker, a district nurse and himself, were

157

asked to visit a referral in a Fulham basement bed-sit. Gloria was described as a 'common' prostitute. She had a five-year-old son, and refused to go into hospital because she had no one to leave him with; she was terrified that he would be taken into care. She screamed at the social worker and wouldn't let her in. Gloria had a fast-growing malignant tumour in her chest cavity and didn't have very long to live, but the doctor had decided that in the circumstances it was probably best for her not to know.

After the initial visit, when they'd cleaned her up and made her comfortable, Steve couldn't get her out of his mind. Her terrible predicament, her fierce protectiveness of her child and the used, defeated beauty of her face haunted him. He came back to see her when he was off duty – the kid was asleep and they talked until four in the morning. He made her something to eat and she made him laugh, and a love of sorts – the kind that blooms rapidly when time is short – sparked between them. He came back the next day and the next, and on Sunday took Gloria and the kid for a drive in the country. That was a happy day and the sun shone, but there was nothing idyllic about the next few weeks. Gloria was a heroin user, a hopelessly self-destructive person caught in a relentless downward spiral. She was unpredictable and moody, with a perverse streak that often seemed to be trying to wound Steve and drive him away. But a dogged stubbornness in him made him keep trying.

Steve had to keep the relationship a secret for fear of losing his job, and the tension was very draining. 'Part of me knew that I wasn't really going to be able to change anything in her life, but I wanted her to know that there was at least one man in the world who wouldn't treat her like a piece of shit,' he said, 'and I loved to see her smile.' He took to staying round there overnight, sleeping on the settee, helping to get the kid off to school in the morning so the social services wouldn't interfere.

Gloria got weaker and weaker but kept denying there was anything seriously the matter with her. One day she told Steve that her greatest dream had always been to spend a romantic weekend in Amsterdam, so he made up his mind to take her there before it was too late. The kid went to stay with Steve's sister and her husband, and Steve booked a room in a little hotel overlooking one of the canals. Gloria cried as she stood at the window and looked out at the misty winter sun caught in the bare branches of the trees and reflected in the surface of the quiet water.

He had never kissed her before but he did now. She felt too ill to make love so they just lay naked together on the bed. He held her in his arms and gently stroked her thin body all over, wincing at the lumpy, bruised needle marks on her arms and the scar where a man had once burned her breast with a cigarette. She curled up like a baby and, in a little child's voice, recalled one or two of the earliest happy memories – she'd had a grandmother who was kind to her and her fourth birthday party had been lovely; she'd worn a new blue dress and a pretend-diamond hair slide.

They had a bath together and drank a bottle of champagne, and Steve brushed her hair in front of the fire. Four days after they returned to London, Gloria died coughing up blood. She was thirty-one years old. Steve wasn't with her and heard the news from someone at the office. 'Remember that hooker . . .?'

Steve had no one he could tell, but a friend who sensed he was at breaking point and thought he just needed a rest had suggested a few days on a Carmelite retreat. This was where Steve had heard of our workshop. Now, only a month after Gloria's death, Steve was sitting with a small group of us sharing his story. He wept constantly, a steady overflow pouring from his eyes. 'I know it's not "professional", not done, to acknowledge feelings,' he said, 'and if you do, it's so hard to deal with them once they flood in. I've managed to keep my feelings under control for years. When I was a policeman I had to deal with traffic accidents, and I once had to break the news to a couple that their missing thirteen-month-old baby had drowned in a neighbour's swimming pool. I coped – after a fashion – but I was falling apart inside.

159

Now I don't want to be like that any more. Caring for Gloria made me human again but it hurts. I've learned that grief is the price you pay for love.'

One of our group, a priest from Northern Ireland, was deeply moved. His voice was husky with emotion as he spoke: 'All I can say is this,' he said. 'Your story has taught me a lot about bringing compassion back into care and I feel privileged to have heard it. When you spoke of your time in Amsterdam I had the clearest picture in my mind of your holding the crucified body of Christ in your arms. You may think you failed Gloria at the end, but what you did was a most wonderful thing. By your love you helped give birth to her into another life.'

It was true, what he said.

'Our powerlessness and vulnerability,' Jean had said, 'are a fact of life. You *cannot* be in control, but whatever you may think about religion, there is no death in nature without a sequel of becoming and resurrection. All we can do is be humble enough to open our hearts. Our own pools of pain are never-ending. All we take with us to someone who is dying is who we are and how clear we can be. Be a conscious participant rather than a bystander,' she urged. 'The strength will be there when you need it. Our strength always comes from the God within us, sometimes reinforced by the love of friends. Take care of yourself. Give to yourself. Modulate your own energy. Be aware of how much you can do and who you want to work with. Ask for support when you need it and you will never burn out.'

Philosophical ideas change nothing by themselves. The trick lies in knowing how to bring great ideas into the heart and into the very tissues of the body. Jean's meditations on opening the heart and breathing someone elses's pain are among the simplest and most effective techniques I have learned.

8

One cannot know the truth, one can only be it.

STEPHEN LEVINE

I recently had a letter from my friend Celine in South Africa. Her forty-one-year-old husband dropped dead on the rugby field from a massive heart attack a couple of years ago, and I had written to ask her if she would tell me some of the things that had been helpful to her in getting through her bereavement. Her response was angry, prickly and dismissive. 'Nothing helps,' she wrote. 'There's nothing you can learn that makes any difference.' She said she felt like a piece of cotton wool totally saturated in black ink. 'Slowly, slowly the ink begins to drain out. Sometimes it sticks, sometimes you can feel it shift a bit and one day you become aware that it has moved through you.' The best thing was to shut up and get on with your life, and 'so-called religion' was worse than useless, she said. 'I can't believe someone up there is *planning* all this.'

I can't accept that someone is planning our suffering either. It's a horrible idea. For me, faith is not so much a question of something you believe in as of something you *are*. A childish concept of God is not helpful in a crisis. If God has let you down, how can you trust anybody? A hospital chaplain told me of the time in Casualty when a man, seeing his priest's dog collar, seized him by the throat and screamed at him, 'Where's your fucking God now? Get down on your knees and pray right this minute! I want a miracle NOW or I'll fucking kill you with my bare hands!' He was deranged with grief, insane with rage because his daughter was dying after a motor-cycle accident. 'There was nothing to be done,' said the chaplain, 'but to watch with him through the pain to a point of restoration.' The man later confessed that the motor-cycle had been a present to his daughter for her sixteenth birthday which he had given her against the better judgement of his wife. His rage was really against himself.

A Hindu priest once said to me: 'I have no ideas about an afterlife. There may be a Christian heaven or a Hindu heaven or there may be nothing at all. The Lord has always been with me and He will be with me when I die.' My own concept of God lies in the understanding that something in me and in everyone I love resides outside the confines of time and space. Buried under the structure of personal fears, wants and needs is an essence – an unchangeable, indivisible, indestructible pure spirit. Just as when you are riding a bicycle, it is trust in your forward motion and trust in your momentum that keeps you from falling. Maybe Celine is right in saying that nothing shortens the mourning period, but I do think it helps to have given some thought to the subject of death before you have to deal with it directly.

One man who had a near-death experience said, 'While completely unique and as individual as a fingerprint, "I" was at the same time part of some ordered, harmonious, infinite whole. It was a reunion, a homecoming. I was remembering something I had known before I was born. I knew in an instant that learning to love people and acquiring higher knowledge were the most important goals in life.'

The aim of any work with dying or bereaved people is to strengthen their sense of the meaning of life. One woman on Jean Sayre-Adams' workshop told me the story of her husband's younger brother, who developed cancer in his early thirties and was determined to conquer it. He tried many self-help tactics and even went to the Philippines to visit a faith healer. 'He died,' she said, 'but by that stage, although it sounds rather strange to say, it didn't matter because he'd won. He and his wife had the most beautiful, serene relationship and he made all the right choices up to the end of his life. In the face of his death he rose to the full stature of his being.

162

He found his own path and sang his own song, and dying took its place in the larger meaning of existence.'

In our world death takes most people by surprise. The traditional supports that used to cradle us in times of need are no longer there. Rites of mourning have fallen into disuse, leaving us in a rather dangerous cultural void. Families drift apart, communities are not constant, and many of us have no religious certainties.

There is no way to put the clock back. But we can learn from the wisdom of past traditions and adapt it to our present needs. Everyone we love will die and sooner or later we will die ourselves. Those are the inescapable facts. To face death is the beginning of mastery over life's terrors:

> If we accept death as necessity rather than strive to demote it to the level of accident, energies now bound up in continuing strivings to shelve the idea of death will be available to us for more constructive aspects of living, perhaps even fortify our gift for creative splendour against our genius for destruction.
>
> HERMAN FEIFEL, *New Meanings of Death*

Life is a difficult and lonely journey for most of us. Its comforts, for the most part, lie in accepting other people and having other people accept us. Everybody has a story to tell and most of us are drowning in the unshed tears of buried grief. A psychologist called Lindeman made some classic studies of those who survived the terrible Coconut Grove fire in America: many young people were burned to death at a disco because the exit doors were padlocked. The studies showed that those who talk and are listened to get better. Somehow we have to find the courage to share our pain and the stillness to hear someone else's. And in the absence of rituals, we must invent our own.

I've been to too many dreary, impersonal, supermarket funerals where the service was droned mechanically as if by a robot. Everything was ugly – canned music, automatic plati-tudes, and nothing of the life that had been lived. The send-off for Claire was very different.

Claire was eight years old when she died of leukaemia. I got to know her and her mother Margot on the children's ward at the Middlesex. Margot and I drank many cups of coffee together in the parents' day room while our children were sleeping, and played many games of Ludo or Catch-a-Mouse when they felt up to it.

A warm, articulate woman, Margot was a wonderful mother, devoting herself patiently and wholeheartedly to making the remainder of Claire's life as rich and full as possible. She talked very movingly about the difficulties faced by the family of a terminally ill child (or adult, for that matter). Everyone was at a different stage of acceptance, anger, depression, denial, and fell out of sync with each other during long periods of remission. 'My husband doesn't want to face the inevitable,' she said gently. 'He just can't bear to talk about it at the moment and makes remarks like "When this nightmare is over . . ." or "When Claire is back at school . . ." My five-year-old has become very callous and detached and says things like "Can I have Claire's bicycle when she dies?" I know it's only his way of defending himself from the pain all around him but I find it hard not to be angry. My ten-year-old has become very withdrawn and started wetting his bed. As for me, I know that this time with Claire is precious but I'm constantly torn between wanting to invest all my energies in hope – hope for a miracle, hope for our continued life together – and needing to disengage myself from her so that she can die when her time comes without feeling guilty about leaving me.'

We kept in touch after leaving hospital. Claire lived for another five months and Margot, through her steadfastness, managed to unite the family at the end; she had good help from the hospital bereavement counsellor, who was very sensitive to the staggering load she was carrying. The funeral, organized magnificently by her husband, was a triumph of life over death. Many children from Claire's old school came, as well as some she'd known in hospital. Their drawings for Claire were stuck up all round the church; drawings of butterflies, flowers and big yellow suns. A few children stood up and read poems. Everyone was given a candle to hold – the place was ablaze with the illuminated faces of children – and a yellow daffodil to throw in the grave.

The minister – a friend of the family – held the little coffin in his arms as he spoke of Claire's courage and of the lightness and joy she'd brought into the world during her short life. The grave was lined with moss and leaves like a nest for a baby bird. We stood with our arms around each other as we threw in an avalanche of daffodils and sang 'The Lord of the Dance' together: 'Dance, dance, wherever you may be . . .' It was the most beautiful funeral I had ever been to and an inspiring example of how it can be. We have begun to reclaim birth and death from the medical profession after generations of abdication – begun to reinstate choice and personal responsibility. Let's do the same with funerals.

A year has passed and Margot has been through some terrible troughs of grief. As she said herself, it's very difficult for friends to get it right. If they keep on coming round to call, she finds herself longing for solitude and the space to grieve in private. If a day goes by and nobody calls she feels desolate and abandoned. 'I'm quite irrational a lot of the time,' she said, 'but the pattern of grief is so unpredictable. Sometimes I cope perfectly well with something I've been dreading, like sorting out Claire's toys. Other times I'll be overwhelmed with misery for no apparent reason while sitting in a bus or something. It seems to well up from nowhere. I've learned there's no "right way" to get through the pain. Everyone does it in their own way, in their own time. The friends who have been the most use are the ones who haven't been afraid to get it wrong. It's better to misjudge the timing than to do nothing at all.

'There's a part of my heart that will always be sad and long for what might have been,' Margot said, 'especially as Claire

165

was my only daugher. I'll miss her more the older she would have been and I'll miss the fun we would have shared and the grandchildren I'll never have, but I am grateful for her life. I'm proud that I was chosen to be her mother and can see the gifts she gave us through her death. I feel sure that at some level her soul chose that life for a reason. She was never afraid of dying, almost as if she knew all along that her time with us would be short.' Margot showed me the last drawing Claire had made and coloured: it was of a little girl in a pale blue dress sitting on a swing which hung from an enormous, brightly coloured rainbow.

Helen House is a hospice for children. At a thanksgiving service to mark its fifth anniversary, the Archbishop of Canterbury gave an address to a gathering of bereaved parents:

The world doesn't quite know what to make of the death of children. Stock phrases are not well geared to handle it. Too often there is talk of lives cut short, as if length of years is what life is really about. You will know and you'll sympathize with people's difficulty in trying to say the right thing. But you will know, too, a greater truth – that no life, however short, is wasted, that no life in which love has been given and received is anything other than complete. There is a Jewish saying which puts what I am attempting to say quite simply: 'There are those who gain eternity in a lifetime, and others who gain it in one brief hour.'

... In their short lives, your children have created much love. Who in the longest life could do more than this? Who could bless us more richly than those who create and leave behind them an atmosphere of love? This is what your children have done, at the cost of much suffering and helplessness, yet also through their suffering and helplessness. I believe that some very ill children realize all this. They become somehow aware that

166

through them love is being created in and among those who care for them. They realize, however indistinctly, that they are doing something very important for their parents, their brothers, their sisters, nurses and friends. They are helping them to love. In doing such a great thing for you, must they not come to love you, just as you, in doing so much for them, love them? I cannot doubt that it is a profound mutual love which is created when great need receives great care . . . And so I believe the love of your child for you still *is*, just as surely and truly as your love for him or her still *is*. Only the suffering of your child has ended, not the love – not the love.

A biography, after all, cannot be judged by the number of pages in it, but only by the richness of the contents, and sometimes the 'unfinished' symphonies are among the most beautiful.

My lovely friends Omega and Djangawu with whom I recently stayed in Australia and from whom I learned much about healing and the ways of the Aborigines, sent me this letter the following year:

Our beautiful son was born at home after eight days of intermittent labour. When he was five days old we had to move into hospital with him. He had Down's Syndrome, a totally blocked bowel and a hole in the heart. I insisted that there be no operation, and we held him, loved him and helped him back to where he came from for one and a half weeks. He died in my arms gently and peacefully. Such a gentle soul. In my time with him, in total attunement, so many areas inside me opened up that may have slept forever. As he died, I grew and grew. What a way to learn. I hope I meet him again . . . Now we plan our lives with more awareness and richness . . . My other boys seem more precious and so is the love and strength we all have together . . .

167

How wise of that little baby to have chosen parents with ears to hear what he had come to teach. He accomplished more in his short life than many people do in fourscore years and ten.

Naomi Grafton wrote this poem for her daughter, who died from a brain tumour at the age of eleven after a sudden, brief illness. I think it distils with great simplicity and eloquence the essence of the gift she brought. It is a celebration and a letting go:

> Precious Louise
> Memories of you sweet child
> Are coloured with laughter
> Tinted with tears
> And your little face comes shining through
>
> Grief is not forever
> But love is.
>
> Was it all a dream
> Dissolved now . . .
> Diffuse mellow memories
> Poignant joyful fragments.
>
> The threads of our lives
> Woven with invisible hands
> Created a beautiful tapestry
> The canvas is now complete.

Hoping to learn more about children and death, I went back to Bristol for a three-day workshop on Death, Dying and Bereavement with Gregg Furth (positively my last death workshop, I promised myself). Gregg Furth is an American psychiatrist best known for the work he has done on the interpretation of spontaneous drawings, particularly those of dying children. Our unconscious minds know a lot more about what's going on inside us than we think – the pale, baby-blue of little Claire's dress in her drawing, for instance, is the colour associated with being whole and in harmony but fading out of life. The rainbow is a symbol of transition, a bridge between one state of being and the next, a covenant between God and man. We can gain access to our own inner knowing by learning to interpret the symbols and metaphors of our drawings, although of course this is not a job for an amateur.

Gregg Furth worked a great deal with Elisabeth Kübler-Ross. Right at the beginning of his career when he was starting to work with dying patients she advised him, 'Don't read case histories. Don't know anything. Ask, "What's happening with you? How can we learn from you to be better doctors? You can teach us."' One patient he went to see laughed and lifted his sheet. 'Look at this body,' he said. 'I'm dying of cancer but they keep taking me for X-rays. I'd like some straight talking.'

'When we know we don't know anything, we know a lot,' said Gregg. There are no answers; Death is such a personal event. But it is useful to make an arena, a forum in which to see what's going on; 'to get conscious about death', as Gregg says. 'Once we realize the extent of our helplessness we can turn around and face it. We can contain helplessness which is very useful.' Sometimes it's very tempting to run, to bury the pain and take off in a frenzy of activity. 'Turn round and face your runner,' says Gregg. 'Stand steady.' This is very good advice and is certainly something I have had to learn in my time working with Lighthouse and as a hospice volunteer. You may not be able to make anyone better, but you can stand steady.

Those two words, more than any others, sum up Gregg's teaching and his personal style. He is very provocative – not lovey-dovey and cuddly like many therapists working in the field of death and bereavement. 'Unconditional love! That's baloney!' he scoffed. 'Unconditional *presence* is what you need. You cannot help a person till you *burn* yourself. It's not so pretty. Meet them where they're really burning. For them, it helps to know someone else is struggling. You've got to *know* about the loneliness, *know* about the fear, and don't be afraid to argue and fight with an old person – it may be the only communication they have.'

169

The course turned out to be quite different from what I'd expected and not really about children, but as John Lennon said, 'Life is what happens to you when you are busy making other plans.'

The emphasis in the second morning's session was on getting the balance right between 'psyche' and 'soma' theories of illness. During the past fifty years, said Gregg, far too much emphasis had been placed on the body, with science as the great panacea, and not enough on the psyche. Now the exact opposite is true. The prevailing tendency is to substitute psychology for medicine. Everybody can be a psychologist. 'The minute you think you have the answer to someone else's psychology you should go and wash your mouth out,' he said. 'You may have the answer to your own but it's never anyone else's answer.'

Looking for a purely psychological explanation for everything is as stupid and wrong as saying that all illness is caused by germs. We run from one side to the other searching for an explanation that will somehow be able to eliminate death.

The essence of Gregg's message was that although you must own your illness, you don't have to feel guilty about having it – you did not cause it. To die is the destiny of all living things. It is the natural and inevitable conclusion to the process of living. In the stampede to pin a psychological explanation to everything we can unwittingly create a tyranny of positive thinking that can lead to a sense of guilt about not getting better.

'Find the middle way,' he said. 'Carry both sides. It's a marriage. Be able to live with the ambiguity, with the paradox, with the unknown. Einstein said: "To stand next to the unanswerable question is to stand next to God." We find it very hard to stand next to unanswerable questions.'

Somebody asked him where suicide came into all this. He talked interestingly about what he called 'the village' – the complex of sub-personalities that go to make us up. Each one of us is a village of priests and thieves, whores and functionaries. Mother Theresa lives there; so does Al Capone. There

170

is a board of directors, a law enforcement officer, and a mayor (the ego). The mayor has to negotiate with the whole complex but often the communications break down. Shadowy figures sometimes sneak out and run riot, figures that the mayor can't control or tolerate. He resigns, and they rip the town apart. 'Find out who it is in the village that wants to die. Mother Theresa doesn't want to die. The whole person doesn't want to die. When someone is threatening to commit suicide, get in and find out who they want to kill.'

Gregg put forward the controversial idea that actually there isn't any other type of death but suicide. Death doesn't just occur to us; it's involved with the whole complex. Some part of us wants out. 'But what about accidents?' somebody asked. 'I've heard people say that there's no such thing as an accident,' he answered. 'That's baloney. Of course there is. We don't set ourselves up on purpose. That would leave the mystery out of the equation – the unanswerable question. There is no easy answer here; we can leave it as an accident or we can look for meaning in it. Synchronicity. The accident happened but why were you there? Things happen to us for a reason. Find out the reason and use it.'

The implication is that all behaviour is meaningful but we often deliberately avoid facing its meaning. We often resist seeing the significance of our behaviour when it comes to our health. Illness and health are both forms of organic behaviour. Deep feelings, even unconscious ones, can be translated into physical symptoms to relieve inner conflict. Karl Menninger (of the Menninger Institute) speaks of illness as a 'flight from frustration and the responsibilities of life' – a retreat into a state of blamelessness. Illness, and ultimately death, can be an accepted and respectable way of dealing with intolerable stress.

We have to hunt, Gregg said, for that sub-personality which we want to kill, that aspect of ourselves we are tired of and hate. When we want to slaughter it, when we say 'I don't want to be a wimp/fatty/coward/pushover/pervert any more,' then the trick is to set up a ceremony to rid ourselves of it.

171

'But *don't ever use it*,' said Gregg. 'Set up a tabernacle to carry it – to contain it. Hate is power. Transcend it. Transform it. Integrate it. Don't annihilate it. If you hate a part of yourself, find out who he or she is and reap the energy. The past still travels with us; it makes us who we are. None of it is bad – it's all useful. Cook on the dung pats. And find out where your guilt lies. The beauty of guilt is that it makes us conscious. You learn for next time. It's hard and painful to be conscious; the task is to figure out what your guilt is trying to make you conscious of.' Whether you agree with him or not, his ideas are very challenging.

We talked about how we deal with the little deaths and losses in our lives because those are the clues to how we are likely to deal with the big ones. In the afternoon, we were all sitting in a circle and Gregg was illustrating some point on the blackboard when it was noticed that one of our group members was missing. 'She's been designated dead,' said Gregg laconically, 'and asked to leave. She has to stay in her room or walk about the grounds but nobody is allowed to talk to her or acknowledge her in any way.' We were outraged, angry, furious with Gregg. 'You have no right. . .!' 'Who do you think you are, playing God?' 'It's so unfair . . . arbitrary . . . unjust . . .' He had made his selection earlier by picking a chair: the first person who sat on it was chosen. 'Death is like that. Unfair. You have no control. It cheats. You don't get your money back,' he responded. One young woman was so angry that she walked out, forfeiting her fee. The whole exercise threw a cat among the pigeons. The squawking went on for a long time and people were extremely upset. I felt a bit uneasy at the way we had all colluded in what the 'authority figure' had ordained, and rather admired the strength and conviction of the person who had left. Nobody really stuck up for her. We acted like people do in real life – feeling relieved that we hadn't got the chop, lying low to see what would happen.

Gregg brazened out the anger that was directed at him. It took some nerve to stand steady but in the end, when everyone had had their say, most people came round to thinking that it was probably a powerful exercise and that Sara, the human sacrifice, would also gain from the experience. The girl who had left had to be allowed to make her own decisions and run if she chose. Trying to stop her or rescue her would not be helpful. 'It really helps a person come to consciousness if you let them run,' said Gregg.

After supper, Sara was resurrected and allowed to return to the group. What she went through felt more like being a person with a terminal illness than being dead, she said. She felt out of things, angry, abandoned, unfairly picked on, ignored, punished, ostracized, talked about behind her back. 'All of you went off to lead your lives without a backward glance at me,' she said. But the exercise had taught her a lot about being isolated and the process of dying. All of us could learn from that. One woman spoke about her eighteen-year-old son who had died the previous year of cancer. Most of his healthy, able-bodied friends fell away during the year of his illness, and on one occasion when he had felt well enough to go on a family walk, everyone else had rushed on ahead leaving only his mother to walk at his pace. Nobody wanted to keep him company.

Gregg read out an anonymous letter from a student nurse first printed in the *American Journal of Nursing* in 1970. It was entitled 'Death in the First Person':

I am a student nurse. I am dying. I write this to you who are, and will become, nurses in the hope that by my sharing my feelings with you, you may someday be better able to help those who share my experience.

I'm out of hospital now – perhaps for a month, for six months, perhaps for a year – but nobody likes to talk about such things. In fact, no one likes to talk about much at all. Nursing must be advancing, but I wish it would hurry. We're taught not to be overly cheery now, to omit the 'Everything's fine' routine, and we have done pretty well. But now one is left in a lonely, silent void.

173

With the protective 'fine, fine' gone, the staff are left with only their own vulnerability and fear. The dying patient is not yet seen as a person and thus cannot be communicated with as such. He is a symbol of what every human fears and what we each know, at least academically, that we too must someday face. What did they say in psychiatric nursing about meeting pathology with pathology to the detriment of both patient and nurse? And there was a lot about knowing one's own feelings before you could help another with his. How true.

But for me, fear is today and dying is now. You slip in and out of my room, give me medications and check my blood pressure. Is it because I am a student nurse myself, or just a human being, that I sense your fright? And your fear enhances mine. Why are you afraid? I am the one who is dying!

I know you feel insecure, don't know what to say, don't know what to do. But please believe me, if you care, you can't go wrong. Just admit that you care. That is really what we search for. We may ask for whys and wherefores, but we don't really expect answers. Don't run away – wait – all I want to know is that there will be someone to hold my hand when I need it. I am afraid. Death may get to be a routine to you, but it is new to me. You may not see me as unique, but I've never died before. To me, once is pretty unique!

You whisper about my youth, but when one is dying, is he really so young any more? I have lots I wish we could talk about. It really would not take more of your time because you are in here quite a bit anyway.

If only we could be honest, both admit of our fears, touch one another. If you really care, would you lose so much of your valuable professionalism if you even cried with me? Just person to person? Then, it might not be so hard to die – in a hospital – with friends close by.

It must be terrible to spend what may be your last few weeks in a context of mutual pretence. It's the 'horse on the dining-room table' syndrome again. Everyone needs open communication and warm personal relationships in order to be able to die well. When Terry was dying at the hospice, a 'good' friend he'd known for years came to visit bearing a large chocolate gâteau. 'Listen,' he said, 'you know how I hate hospitals. They always make me depressed so I won't stay, but I've brought you this to nibble.' Then he disappeared, leaving the obscene cake on the bedside locker. Terry, at that time, weighed about four stone and hadn't eaten for a week.

'The most important, the only thing a fellow human being can do is dare to accompany feelings,' said Gregg. This perfectly endorsed the experience and teaching of Jean Sayre-Adams. When Ram Dass sat with her through her great suffering he wasn't trying to change anything, say anything, offer anything; he was simply daring to accompany her.

In the afternoon we concentrated on ways of completing grief, on the need for ritual and what it accomplishes. Rituals work at unconscious and conscious levels, said Gregg. They are a way of saying a great deal in a little time, in a language deeper than words, and of making a person feel connected to something greater than himself. They are the literal and symbolic means by which we leave something behind and allow ourselves to move on. Ritual is crucial to letting things go.

One woman told of the death of her baby, one of twins. As in the case of many neonatal deaths in those days, the baby was unceremoniously disposed of in the hospital incinerator. She never held him; she had no photograph of him and not a single memento. Her doctor told her to stop feeling sorry for herself. She was lucky to have the other one, he said, and gave her tranquillizers. For years she suppressed the fact of his death and her feelings about it in the same way as Jean had – to the detriment of her mental and physical health. Finally she managed to bring him back into focus, back from the doldrums where he was becalmed in the sea of her unconscious mind. She was able to talk to him, talk about him, have a funeral service and a little ritual to fill his sails with wind, say

175

goodbye and blow him on his way ... twenty-seven years after his death. 'The spirit is not released until you let go,' said Gregg, 'and the dumbest thing we do is to give anti-depressants.'

Although insensitivity is still, alas, not unusual, a much more enlightened attitude prevails today: a baby who is stillborn or only lives a short while is respected not as a person who might have been but as one who *is*. When my neighbour's baby was stillborn, she and her husband were treated with great kindness and care. They were encouraged to name the baby, hold her, dress her in something pretty, and have a proper funeral service to which the other children in the family came. Nothing was rushed – there was all the time in the world. She was acknowledged as a human being, a precious guest who couldn't stay. She was greeted, made welcome, loved and mourned.

The great thing about rituals is that it is never too late to perform them. Even years after the event, the fear, anger, guilt or sadness that has been festering away can finally be let go. We were asked to sit down and write a letter to someone in our lives who had died.

I wrote to my grandfather, whom I had never met. The letter flowed easily and lucidly without unearthing too much emotion, but when each of us was asked to read our letter to a partner, who had to sit quietly and listen, it was quite a different matter. Hearing the words read aloud and seeing them set down on paper brought up all the feelings that had been buried since my childhood. I couldn't get through it without choking on my tears.

To my beloved and unknown grandfather

I only have one photograph of you – kind-looking, bearded, so foreign and yet part of me. I expect you would be shocked by how much the world has changed and how your deeply held traditions have dispersed. I, your first grandchild with my auburn hair and green eyes, married to a blond Anglo-Saxon with our strange mixture of children – your great-grandchildren, African and English. How little we would have in common on the surface but how much of me comes from the person I believe you were.

I don't even know how old you were when you were murdered – probably not much older than I am now, but I do know how your best qualities lived on in your only son, your precious boychick, your thin little Rachmil who survived against all the odds and carried the inner rivers away across the world to merge with other currents full of vigour and life.

Your Fiddler-On-The-Roof, medieval way of life is no longer, but everything you stood for is still safe. Daddy talked about you whenever he could bear to remember. I knew the story of your stark and violent death. I knew how saintly and good you were as a human being – bringing home tramps for a meal, giving too much change to poor people in your shop, sharing your belongings.

You have never been forgotten. Although your grave in Poland was desecrated, we erected a tablet for you next to daddy in the Jewish cemetery here in London. Actually it was mum who wanted to do that. Your son's 'shicksa' wife who carried the flame more than anyone.

If you want to know about me – I am well and happy and full of loving. Your son was a wonderful father and I miss him a lot – his physical presence, that is. I always feel his spirit which is absorbed into me.

I really wish I could have met you, had a Friday night dinner in your house, shared a Passover Seder. I wish I had one memento from your life – a candlestick or something. But there is nothing material left – all gone. The house, the village, the people, the things. What remains is the singing and I hear that in my heart, and the photograph which I keep in my English house next to my other grandparents whom I also never knew – John Moore, the defrocked clergyman and his beautiful, reckless actress wife. Wouldn't you have been surprised at the company you now keep?

You have a great-great-grandson, little Julian David, and another on the way. You did not die. Don't be distressed by the dilution of the religious orthodoxy. It hasn't damaged God at all. Our consciousness is evolving at a very rapid rate and different words are used to try and give expression to the divine and spiritual dimension in our lives. The truth is not harmed but remains, as it always was, notoriously difficult to pin down in language.

You and I shared no common tongue and would not have been able to speak to each other in words, but I feel you in my heart and in the innermost rivers of my being.

Know that I remember you, respect you and love you.

Lalushka

Some people wrote angry letters, some sad, some sorry. One man wrote to his father but also realized, halfway through, that it was really his mother, still living, to whom he wanted to address his anger. 'Where the fuck were you when all this abuse was going on? Why didn't you protect me?' One woman wrote to her stillborn child; another to her brother who was killed in a road accident; another to her young son who died fourteen years ago – 'The anguished young mother will never go away even though there are parts of me that are fine . . .'

There were a lot of tears in the room as the letters were read. My partner, Anne, a woman in her early fifties, had written to her father, who was taken as a prisoner of war by the Japanese; he had never been able to show her any affection at the best of times and became very withdrawn and remote after his release. Anne has had a very hard life with multiple losses; the infant death of her first child; a divorce; the death of her lover; the death from a brain tumour of her beloved son Ian, at the age of twenty-five; the deaths of both her parents within four months of each other; and finally her own serious skiing accident two years ago which has left her crippled and in pain. Being very British and coming from a tradition of stiff upper lips where crying was a sign of weakness, she has always found it very difficult to release her emotions. She only grieved

178

properly for her son, she said, when she began to mourn her leg; then all the sadness of a lifetime came pouring out. I was very moved by her letter to her father, which perfectly captured her poignant longing for his love and the bitterness she is still exorcising:

My darling Daddy,

I felt very privileged to be with you when you died. To me it was a wonderment and a kind of miracle that you let go as I put the crumb of communion bread dipped in wine into your mouth. There was an extraordinary sense of peace in the room as your last breath was breathed softly out, and Mummy and I blessed you with our love and our goodbyes.

I was glad, so glad, I had the courage to tell you you were dying the day before, even though I knew you did not really want to hear it, and to ask you if there was anything you wanted to say to us. I longed for you to say goodbye in some way to me, to tell me that you loved me, that in spite of all the difficulties we had had, I meant a lot to you, that as your only daughter I was precious. But you never did. You only asked for Robert, not for me.

I've loved you, Daddy, all my life. As a little girl I idolized you, and then you sent me away at five years old to boarding school. Far away into the mountains. I felt completely abandoned and unloved and UNWANTED. Unwanted – that has haunted me all my life. I remember walking up the platform in Singapore to the train at 10.00 at night, dressed in my pyjamas, holding both your and Mummy's hands and crying, crying, crying – always crying – 'no one loves me, no one wants me.'

Did you love me? Did you want me? I think, in fact I know, you did, from what other people told me you said about me, but why didn't you *tell me?* I missed you desperately while you were a prisoner of war, and then while I was at boarding school in England and you were out in Malaya again. Did you know what happened to

179

me in the holidays? Did you know how I was passed around the family and friends like a parcel – to be left with whoever would be prepared to take me? I had to find methods of survival – and probably in my life they have served me well, but they were not methods I would have chosen.

In your last years it was I who cared for you and Mummy, I who loved and supported you, it was my children who came to cut your grass, weed the garden, pick the apples, make your birthday cake. Do you remember that? Yet it was always Robert's family and Avril his wife most of all whom you showered with your attention. Their children drank, smoked and talked at parties while mine worked in the kitchen doing the preparation and washing up. It was the same with me.

I don't know whether I shall ever really forgive you for refusing me financial help when Ian was diagnosed with a terminal illness and I had to give up my job – even when I asked you directly. I was desperate for help and you said 'no'. Later you gave it to me under Mummy's pressure, but you put conditions on it – I mustn't tell Robert you had given it to me. I know you remmebered it because later that year you said it was alright to talk about it – Robert and Avril needed a new car and you had given them £2000 for it. It absolved your conscience but what about my feelings? For me it was a matter of survival for my dying child, for them it was a luxury. What do you think about that now? And the time you refused to lend me your Saab to take him to hospital in because you had an appointment to have your hair cut. I felt utterly rejected and furious. I never had the courage to tell you that but I'm telling you now.

In spite of it, we all loved you and showed it. After my accident when you and Mummy became more frail, I was determined to help and support you enough with organized help to keep you in your own home. It was hard when I was struggling on crutches but I am glad that I

180

enabled you and Mummy to die at home in your own
beds with your family around you. You never went to a
home or a hospital – I fought for you, I kept my faith
with you, whom I loved so much.

Your daughter,
Anne

Poetry, and indeed, drawing, painting, song, dance – the
artistic and creative impulses which enable us to give expression
to our deepest feelings – are also powerful ways to transform
grief into insight, enabling us to move on. This is a poem to her
father by my friend Mary Sheepshanks. To me, it conveys with
subtlety and compassion all the complexities of a difficult man.
A fine synthesis of observation, love, understanding, acceptance
and forgiveness, it is above all a self-healing.

Time To Straighten Your Tie

Be careful with prayers: they can be dangerous,
ignite unexpectedly. Perhaps they should carry a
    Government Health Warning.

Hearing of your friend's death,
a sudden seizure while dropping a dry-fly
over a rising trout,
I said:
        'Oh Pa, wouldn't you like
to go like that? To cease mid-stream,
mid-cast, no long farewell?'
You were horrified. Not for you such untidy impulse of
    departure.
'That is not how I want to die,'
you said.
        'Before I meet my Maker
I would like time to straighten my tie.'

And it was granted you!
Oh it was granted you,

181

this wish, this dangerous prayer:
two long painful years, while the flesh
was slowly honed down to the bones,
and your tie was straight,
so very straight.

You showed me much: the values of integrity,
humility, unfailing courtesy . . . the brash
could bark their shins on your politeness . . .
and you were master of the soft answer
that may turn wrath away, but can annoy.
Old-fashioned virtues, yours, but not
the worse for that.
If you were too fastidious for compassion,
which is essentially an earthy thing,
you were still quite exceptionally kind.
Your wit was a kingfisher's beak, your humour
syncopated rhythm. You showed me words:
always inset meter, patterned rhyme,
but words that had a ring.
You did not teach me how to have a fling.

Was it a comfort to you, your faithful
disciplined, pew-steady Churchianity?
I really do not know: support, possibly yes,
but comfort, sadly no. If consciousness
survives the jumble-sale disposal in the earth
I hope you get a wonderful surprise.

I hope some infinitely gentle Angel
(surely not God, who must be hierarchies on)
greeted you. I hope it said:
'My dear chap! How lovely to see you!
You must be quite exhausted. Come on in.'
I hope it said: 'Your laces look a bit too straight,
do slacken them a bit, we're quite informal here.'

Was it like this? And did the Angel say:
'Judgement Day. There's no such thing.
It's D.I.Y. You've judged yourself so hard
these last two years. Besides we're modern here:
Continuous Assessment; not exams.
Sin? Why yes, perhaps you ought
to learn to sin a little bit,
you who were always so afraid of it.
There are a few harmless ones that you might care
to re-evaluate sometime. But later, not just yet.
You are so tired, and we're so very pleased
to see you.'

Was it like that?
I'd like to think it so.
But then alas,
I really do not know.

We could, if we so wished, make an envelope for our letters
and 'post' them in a bonfire. Not to destroy them, said Gregg,
but to use burning as transformation. Smoke can travel to
another world. Ashes can scatter on the wind.

A ritual helps you make a transition in your life. It contains
within it the seeds which enable you to take responsibility for
your own life and for the choices you make. It provides the
support, the solidarity and the symbolism to help you go on
to another stage of development. It marks the death of one
phase and the birth of another.

The chaplain at my hospice once told me about a distraught
widower who wanted to celebrate his dead wife's birthday at
her graveside but was told by his local vicar that it would be
totally inappropriate, in poor taste and extremely morbid. He
died in a mental hospital less than a year later. Maybe he
would have died anyway; but I think we should be much more
aware of the importance of ceremonies and rites of passage.
They are very healing.

Judy Tatelbaum writes in her helpful book *The Courage to*

Grieve: 'Grief is a wound that needs attention in order to heal. To work through and complete grief means to face our feelings openly and honestly, to express and release our feelings fully and to tolerate and accept our feelings for however long it takes for the wound to heal. We fear that once acknowledged grief will bowl us over. The truth is that grief experienced does dissolve. Grief unexpressed is grief that lasts indefinitely.'

And at little Claire's funeral service, the minister said: 'Bereavement is the deepest initiation into the mysteries of human life, an initiation more searching and profound than even happy love. Love remembered and consecrated by grief belongs more clearly than anything to the eternal world: It has proved stronger than death.'

The most moving tale of transition and transformation I ever heard was told by Robert White, an American factory worker from North Carolina.

The story had begun when Robert and his wife went to visit their daughter Lee in hospital as they did every evening.

'It's not easy to die when you are fifteen, but Lee had already accepted her fate,' said Robert. As he spoke, his eyes were full of tears and he could barely keep his voice steady. 'She knew she had an illness that would not spare her. She knew that in spite of their finest efforts the doctors couldn't save her. She suffered a lot but never complained. This particular evening she seemed tranquil and composed but suddenly she said, "Mama, daddy – I think I'm going to die soon and I'm afraid. I know I'm going to a better world than this one and I'm longing for some peace at last but it's hard to accept the idea that I'm going to die at only fifteen."

'We could have lied, telling her of course she wasn't going to die, but we didn't have the heart. Somehow her courage was worth more than our pretence. We just cuddled her and cried together. Then she said, "I always dreamed of falling in love, getting married, having kids . . . but above all I would have liked to work in a big marine park with dolphins. I've loved them and wanted to know more about them since I was little. I still dream of swimming with them free and happy in the open sea." She'd never asked for anything, but now she said with all the strength she could muster, "Daddy, I want to swim in the open sea among the dolphins just once. Maybe then I wouldn't be so scared of dying."

'It seemed like an absurd, impossible dream but she, who had given up just about everything else, hung on to it.

'My wife and I talked it over and decided to do everything we could. We had heard of a research centre in the Florida Keys and we phoned them. "Come at once," they said. But that was easier said than done. Lee's illness had used up all our savings and we had no idea how we would be able to afford air tickets to Florida. Then our six-year-old, Emily, mentioned that she'd seen something on television about a foundation that grants the wishes of very sick children. She'd actually written down the telephone number in her diary because it seemed like magic to her.

'I didn't want to listen. I thought it sounded like a fairy tale or a very sick joke and I gave in only when Emily started crying and accusing me of not really wanting to help Lee. So I phoned the number and three days later we were all on our way. Emily felt a bit like a fairy god-mother who had solved all our problems with a wave of her magic wand.

'When we arrived at Grass Key, Lee was pale and terribly thin. The chemotherapy she'd been having had made all her hair fall out and she looked ghastly, but she didn't want to rest for a minute and begged us to take her straight away to the dolphins. It was an unforgettable scene. When she got into the water, Lee was already so weak she hardly had the strength to move. We had put her in a wet suit so she wouldn't get cold and a life preserver to keep her afloat.

'I towed her out toward the two dolphins, Nat and Tursi, who were frolicking around about thirty feet away from us. At first they seemed distracted and uninterested but when Lee called them softly by name they responded without hesitation. Nat came over first, raised his head and gave her a kiss on the

185

end of her nose. Then Tursi came over and greeted her with a flurry of little high-pitched squeaks of joy. A second later they picked her up with their mighty fins and carried her out to sea with them.

"It feels like I'm flying!" cried Lee, laughing with delight. I hadn't heard her laugh like that since before she became ill. I could hardly believe it was true, but there she was gripping Nat's fin and challenging the wind and the immensity of the ocean. The dolphins stayed with Lee for more than an hour, always tender, always attentive, never using any unnecessary force, always responsive to her wishes.

'Maybe it's true that they are more intelligent and sensitive creatures than man. I know for certain that those marvellous dolphins understood that Lee was dying and wanted to console her as she faced her great journey into the unknown. From the moment they took her in hand they never left her alone for a second. They got her to play and obeyed her commands with a sweetness that was magical. In their company Lee found for one last time the enthusiasm and the will to live. She was strong and happy like she used to be. At one point she shouted, "The dolphins have healed me, daddy!"

'There are no words to describe the effect that swim had on her. When she got out of the water it was as if she had been reborn.

'The next day she was too weak to get out of bed. She didn't even want to talk, but when I took her hand she squeezed it and whispered, "Daddy, don't be sad for me. I'll never be afraid again. The dolphins have made me understand that I have nothing to fear." Then she said, "I know I'm going to die tonight. Promise me that you'll cremate my body and scatter my ashes in the sea where the dolphins swim. They gave me the most beautiful moments of my life. They have left me with a great feeling of peace in my heart and I know they will be with me on the long journey that lies ahead." Just before dawn she woke and said, "Hold me, daddy, I'm so cold." And she died like that in my arms a few minutes later –

186

passing from sleep to death without a ripple. I only realized her suffering was over because her body became colder and heavier.

'We cremated her as she wanted and went out the next day to scatter her ashes in the ocean amongst the dolphins. We were all crying, I'm not ashamed to say; not just my wife and I and our three other children, but even the sailors on the boat that had taken us out into the bay. Suddenly, through our tears, we saw the great arching silver shapes of Nat and Tursi leaping out of the water ahead of us. They had come to take our daughter home.'

To help someone invent their own celebrations and live out their dreams is the finest gift the human heart can bestow.

. . . and all in the end is harvest.

FURTHER READING

Ariès, Philippe, *Western Attitudes to Death* (1976)

Christie, Anne, *A Time to Weep* (1987)

Dass, Ram and Paul Gorman, *How Can I Help?* (1985)

Enright, D J, *The Oxford Book of Death* (Oxford, 1983)

Erikson, Erik, *Insight and Responsibility* (New York, 1964)

Fabian, Ailsa, *The Daniel Dairy* (1988)

Feifel, Herman, *New Meanings of Death* (New York, 1977)

Frankl, Viktor, *Man's Search for Meaning* (New York, 1959)

Fromm, Erich, *The Fear of Freedom* (1960)

Grey, Margot, *Return From Death* (1985)

Grof, Stanislav, and Christina Grof, *Beyond Death* (1980)

Grof, Stanislav, and Joan Halifax, *The Human Encounter With Death* (New York, 1977)

Hill, Susan, *In the Springtime of the Year* (1974)

Hinton, John, *Dying* (1971)

Jackson, Edgar *(et al.)*, *Counselling the Dying* (1982)

Jung, C G, *Man and His Symbols* (1964)

Jung, C G, *Memories, Dreams, Reflections* (1977)

Kübler-Ross, Elisabeth, *AIDS: The Ultimate Challenge* (1988)

Kübler-Ross, Elisabeth, *On Children and Death* (1984)

Kübler-Ross, Elisabeth, *On Death and Dying* (1970)

Kübler-Ross, Elisabeth, *Death: The Final Stage of Growth* (New Jersey, 1978)

Kübler-Ross, Elisabeth, *To Live Until We Say Goodbye* (New Jersey, 1978)

Kübler-Ross, Elisabeth, *Working It Through* (1982)

Kushner, Harold, *When Bad Things Happen to Good People* (1982)

Levine, Stephen, *A Gradual Awakening* (New York, 1979)

Levine, Stephen, *Meetings at the Edge* (New York, 1984)

Levine, Stephen, *Who Dies?* (New York, 1982)

Lewis, C S, *A Grief Observed* (1966)

Lorimer, David, *Survival? Body, Mind and Death in the Light of Psychic Experience* (1984)

Manning, Margaret, *The Hospice Alternative* (1984)

Moody, Raymond, *Life after Life* (1975)

Moody, Raymond, *Reflections on Life After Life* (1978)

Mullin, Glenn, *Death and Dying: The Tibetan Tradition* (1986)

Pincus, Lily, *Death in the Family* (1981)

Rajneesh, Bhagwan Shree, *The Art of Dying* (1980)

Ring, Kenneth, *Heading Towards Omega* (New York, 1984)

Saunders, Cicely, *Beyond All Pain* (1983)

Saunders, Cicely, and Mary Baines, *Living with Dying* (Oxford, 1983)

Siegal, Bernie, *Love, Medicine and Miracles* (1986)

Spence, Christopher, *AIDS: Time to Reclaim Our Power* (1986)

Tatchell, Peter, *AIDS: A Guide to Survival* (1986)

Tatelbaum, Judy, *The Courage to Grieve* (1986)

Trueman, Jill, *Letter to My Husband* (1988)

Winn, Denise, *The Hospice Way* (1987)

USEFUL ADDRESSES

Cancer Help Centre
Grove House
Cornwallis Road
Clifton
Bristol BS8 4PG

Compassionate Friends
5 Lower Clifton Hill
Clifton
Bristol
Avon
(self-help groups for bereaved
parents)

Cruse
Cruse House
126 Sheen Road
Richmond
Surrey TW9 1UR
(support for widows, widowers
and their children)

Hospice Information Service
St Christopher's Hospice
Lawrie Park Road
London SE26 6DZ

London Lighthouse
111-17 Lancaster Road
London W11 1QT

Nicheren Shoshu UK
(Japanese Buddhist Centre)
1 The Green
Richmond
Surrey

Open Gate Trust
6 Goldney Road
Clifton
Bristol BS8 4RB
(lectures and courses on all
aspects of healing and spiritual
development)

Rigpa (Tibetan Buddhist
Centre)
44 St Paul's Crescent
London NW1 9TN

Shanti Nilaya
PO Box 212
London NW8 7NW
(for information on Elisabeth
Kübler-Ross's work)

Wrekin Trust
Runnings Park
Croft Bank
Malvern
Worcestershire WR14 4BP
(lectures and courses on all
aspects of healing and spiritual
development)